NORTHERN IRELAND
OUR LESSER KNOWN HISTORY

A Reprint of 'Sketches of Olden Days in Northern Ireland' by

CANON HUGH FORDE

NORTHERN IRELAND - OUR LESSER KNOWN HISTORY
Sketches of Olden Days in Northern Ireland by Canon Hugh Forde

First published, 1926
This edition 2015

Published by Bannside Library Ltd
135-139 Upper Newtownards Road,
Belfast, BT4 3HX
Northern Ireland

ISBN 978-0-9934157-0-8

Printed by TH Jordan Ltd.
1a Millar Street, Belfast, BT6 8JZ
+44 (0)28 9045 0866
www.thjordanltd.com

Bannside Library Ltd
135-139 Upper Newtownards Road,
Belfast, BT4 3HX
Northern Ireland

Ian aged 12

Ian and Harold

Gospel Tabernacle

Waveney Road, Ballymena

Sunday School

To. *IAN PAISLEY*
SPECIAL

PRIZE

For Attendance 1937

Pastor J. K. Paisley

The original cover of the book along with the presentation page.

"Thus shall memory often, in dreams sublime,
Catch a glimpse of the days that are over;
Thus, sighing, look through the waves of time
For the long-faded glories they cover."

A Note to Readers

THE Right Hon. Sir James Craig wrote the Foreword for this book by Rev Canon Hugh Forde.

He dated it 17 March, 1926.

Just under one month later on 6 April, 1926 my husband was born, and when he was eleven years of age he received a copy of it as a Sunday School prize.

We have reproduced the certificate which is still on his copy of the book.

You will also see he later embellished it with a sticker - an enduring love of youngsters even in this digital age! The sticker is from the Empire Exhibitions which were held in 1938 and included Scotland and Ireland. For a then 12 year old boy they must have been a fascination.

When planning the opening of his personal Library for public access, Ian chose to reproduce this book to mark the occasion. He felt it was universal in appeal and a timely reminder of how greatly we need to treasure our rich inheritance and teach its cultural wealth to the next generation.

EILEEN PAISLEY
BARONESS OF ST. GEORGE'S
Bannside Library, Belfast.
September 2015

TRIBUTE

By Dr Ian Adamson OBE

IT is a great privilege for me to write a Tribute for this little book on the history of Ulster placenames, a Sunday School prize which was treasured by my friend Rev Dr Ian Paisley, the Lord Bannside PC. I do this both in honour and in tribute to him. I was his Personal Adviser on History and Culture from July 2004 until his death on 12th September, 2014. Indeed a very close friend of both Dr Paisley and his family, I was deeply affected by his final illness and passing from this world to the next.

His great oratory and acute perception of the human condition made him the most prominent British politician of the second half of the 20th Century. But I will remember him particularly as a wonderful travelling companion to the bookshops we visited regularly both here and in Great Britain. He loved his books and his magnificent library. He was indeed the most intelligent and widely-read person I had ever met, a kindly and responsive man, for whom no request for assistance ever went unheeded.

On New Year's Day 1985, Dr Paisley presented me with two special volumes from that library which he had himself written, America's Debt to Ulster and The Massacre of St Bartholomew. These two historical treatises he loved, the latter, especially as Eileen was of Huguenot descent. The history of Edward Carson and James Craig were also of special interest to him and he gave me a valuable photographic collection on the subject. And, of course, we cannot forget his deep knowledge of Derry, Aughrim, Enniskillen and the Boyne.

On 1st July 1986, under the auspices of Rhonda, then Lady Mayoress of Belfast, we held a Press Conference to launch, through the Farset organization, what was to become the Somme Association. At this event in Belfast City Hall, Dr Paisley explained his position as a European MP and committed himself to help us refurbish the Ulster Tower at Thiepval in France and open a museum both there and at Conlig, County Down, where the original Helen's Tower stands. He emphasised that this was a project to honour everyone who had fought at the Somme, both Unionist and Nationalist, Roman Catholic and Protestant.

When he and Rev David McIlveen went on missionary work to the Cameroon, I gave them their Yellow Fever vaccinations. Dr Paisley became very ill on one occasion and I diagnosed him as having West Nile Fever. For the Christmas of 1987 he therefore gave to me his two volume edition of Rev J. A. Wylie's 'The History of Protestantism', inscribed by him, *'To Dr Ian, with best thanks for injecting me, medicine and history !!!'*

Following this, in 1992, he made representations to the government to help me set up the Ullans or Ulster-Scots Academy which was predicated on the preservation of Ullans, Ulidian or Ulster Gaelic, and Ulster English, including Belfast English, as well as the history of Dalriada, Dalaradia, Dal Fiatach, Galloway and Carrick, much of which you will read in this book.

But it was the history of early Christianity in the British Isles which became the focus of his work with the Ullans Academy. Dr Paisley and Eileen, now Baroness Paisley, were our principal guests at the St Patrick's Breakfast and Feast of Columbanus events we held regularly, his speeches demonstrating the incomparable grasp he had of a subject he held so dearly in his heart. A second Columbanus himself, his long and fruitful life had as its guiding principle his abiding love and worship of his Master Jesus. All his activities were subordinate to this one ideal and through it he worked out his Salvation by the wondrous pathway that he knew. He was a politician only by circumstance, a theologian by vocation, a contemplative man driven to action by the evils of this world, a Pilgrim on the Road to Paradise. He has arrived home at last. Christ loved Ian Paisley…Well too, did he, the Lord.

DR IAN ADAMSON OBE
Cultra
September 2015

FOREWORD

By Rt. Hon. Sir James Craig

IN commending these brilliant sketches to the people of Ulster, and to visitors to our shores, I do so with all the more pleasure because, although our native country is teeming with historical interest and is well supplied with ancient monuments, suitable books of reference are comparatively few.

Canon Forde has done a public service in compiling so accurate a record of Olden Days, and providing an interesting glimpse of the life led by Ulstermen of bygone times.

It may be somewhat outside the scope of a foreword, but the excellence of this work nerves me to express the hope that Canon Forde will continue to add to his admirable series, of which this is the second edition.

If other readers enjoy as much as I have done a perusal of the present work, they will indeed feel grateful to the distinguished Ulsterman, The Author.

I congratulate him most heartily upon his able treatment of a subject close to the lives and hearts of the people of the Imperial Province.

James Craig.

Stormont Castle,
ULSTER, March 17, 1926.

LIST OF CONTENTS

PART ONE
HISTORICAL NOTES

PART TWO
ON THE SEA COAST OF DERRY, ANTRIM AND DOWN

PART ONE
HISTORICAL NOTES

ULSTER IN THE EARLY CENTURIES

DOWN to the Christian era both Britain and Ireland were regarded on the continent as Pictish rather than Celtic countries. The earliest notice of Ireland is by a Greek, Poseidonius, about 150 B.C. Irish heroic tradition, Sir Samuel Ferguson tells us, revolves in two cycles, separated by an interval of almost two and a half centuries. In the first, beginning about the commencement of the Christian era, Conor, King of Ulster, occupies the central place, surrounded by Cuchulain, Conal Cearnach, and the heroes of the Red Branch. In the second cycle Cormac Mac Art must be regarded as the central figure, though eclipsed by the more heroic forms of Finn and Oisin. The Red Branch Knights were a band of warriors in the service of Conchobar Mac Nessa, King of Ulster. The Palace of Conchobar was situated about three miles west of the present city of Armagh. The name of the ancient fort was Emain or Emain Macha. The huge fort still exists, and it extends over more than eleven acres of land. From Cormac MacArt, who founded the monarchy of Tara about A.D. 250, descended a line of kings who preserved to the year A.D. 1000 a practically unbroken succession in the high kingship. The Kingdom of Ireland was already nine centuries old before the Normans

came, and up to that time was purely Gaelic. Nial of the Nine
Hostages, a descendant of Cormac MacArt, was King of Tara
about A.D. 400.

Three of the sons of this powerful monarch- Eogan, Conall,
and Enna-carved out principalities for themselves in Ulster,
which bore their names for centuries - Tir Conaill, or, as it was
later in English, Tyrconnell, the land of Conaill; and Tir Eogan,
the land of Eogan, from which has come the name of one of the
Ulster counties-Tyrone. Eogan's Land was held by the mighty
fortress of Ailech, a few miles from the city of Derry, which is
still among the chief wonders of Ireland, with its central
enclosure of 77 feet in diameter, surrounded by a wall of
uncemented stones, and hidden galleries and passages to secret
entrances.

From this stronghold, commanding the two great waterways
of Lough Foyle and Lough Swilly, ruled the Kings of Ailech or
Kings of Focha-an old Irish word for the North. In Belmont,
close to Derry, there is a much venerated piece of antiquity-St.
Columba's Stone-generally believed to have been the coronation
stone of Ailech. In the "Tripartite Life of St. Patrick" mention
is made of this stone: "The man of God accompanied Prince
Eochan to his palace, which he then held in the most ancient
and cultivated seat of the kings called Aileach, and which the
holy bishop consecrated, promising that from his seed many
kings and princes of Ireland should spring, and as a pledge he
left there a certain stone, blessed by him, upon which the
promised kings and princes should be crowned." The stone is a
rough, unhewn slate, of an irregular square about seven feet
across. It exhibits the impression of two feet about ten inches
long. There is a very exact description of such coronation stones
in Spenser's "View of the State of Ireland, 1596," which applies
exactly to this stone, which is highly venerated.

For a thousand years the native Gaelic kings held sway in
Ireland, till their power was shattered by the Norman invasion
of 1167 to 1172. The country during this period became a great

centre of learning; students came to its schools in Bangor, Armagh, Downpatrick, Dungiven, and other centres from abroad; it produced and sent all over Europe some very remarkable men-St. Columbanus to Italy, St. Gall to Switzerland, St. Kilian to France, St. Sivin to Belgium, all of whom were pioneers of learning, civilisation, and Christianity. Ireland came to be known as the Island of Saints and Scholars.

The annals and the historical tracts of these times are abundant. The national epics were collected together in the Book of Leinster, A.D. 1150, and other book selections which have not survived. Many ancient writings were lost through the destruction and mutilation of the Danes when they ravaged the land. That they destroyed these books, and did not take them away, is confirmed by the fact that not a fragment of any such manuscript has as yet been found among the collection of the ancient records of Copenhagen. Another cause of the loss of these documents was the occurrence of the Anglo-Norman invasion so soon after the expulsion of the Danes.

When we come down to the thirteenth century we find there is little or no history common to the whole of Ireland. Each province, and even smaller district, must be treated separately; for though there was a central government, nominally supreme over all, its influence and activities, while fully maintained in some parts, were almost unfelt in others. The affairs of each province were in general little affected by events outside its borders. This aloofness of certain districts is particularly true of Ulster, Mr. Orpen tells us. Indeed, it is noteworthy that throughout the whole historical period the people of Ulster, broadly speaking, kept very much to themselves, and, except on rare occasions, interfered but seldom with the rest of Ireland; yet, both in legendary and historical pictures, their pre-eminence as warriors is acknowledged. Even when the nominal Ard-ri was no longer, as a matter of course, one of the race of Niall Mor, they never, except perhaps momentarily, submitted to any other aspirant to the head kingship. When King Henry II came to Ireland, the Ultonian or Northern princes scorned to offer their submission; and although that fearless Norman fighter, John De Courcy, forced the Ulidian princes of north-east Ulster to submit to him, the great clan group of the rest of the province continued to preserve their independence in a marked degree.

This isolation and independence of control is even more noticeable in the thirteenth century under Norman rule in Ulster. First we see the knight John De Courcy- "Princeps Ulidiæ," as Jocelyn calls him- reigning in part of Ulster like an independent king. At length he is displaced by Hugh De Lacey at the bidding of King John, whom he had flouted; but the king soon finds that Hugh De Lacey is not more amenable to control than his predecessor, and he has to lead a great expedition in person to expel the earl he has created.

So, again, when the earldom of Ulster is renewed in the person of the De Burgh, Norman Ulster stands aloof from Ireland, and Ireland from her. Richard De Burgh succeeded his father, Walter. He was known as the "Red Earl." In his time, up to the year 1315, there was comparative peace in the Province of Ulster, and the Red Earl exercised a power never previously surpassed by any ruler of Ulster, and he seems, in general, to have exercised it with moderation. It looked as if the pax Normanica was at last beginning to extend over the entire North of Ireland; but the insecure fabric of Norman rule was shaken to its foundation by the Scottish invasion of Ireland by Edward Bruce in 1315, and finally fell with the fall of the house of De Burgh.

The Irish chiefs of the O'Neill clan once more came into power, and Shane O'Neill for a time became the undisputed master of Ulster. Years after, in the days of one of his descendants-Con O'Neill-through a paltry quarrel, the influence of this powerful family waned, and the way was opened for the Scottish settlement of County Down, and, soon after, for the Plantation of Ulster by King James I.

THE PASSING OF THE O'NEILLS OF CLANABOYE

ABOUT the beginning of the sixteenth century the O'Neills of Clanaboye were a powerful clan. The sept had all along been opposed to the English, and had forfeited their baronial rights, but in 1552 Hugh O'Neill of Clanaboye promised allegiance to the reigning sovereign, and obtained the castle of Carrickfergus, the town and fortress of Belfast, and all the surrounding lands. When Queen Elizabeth came to the throne Phelim O'Neill was the head of the family, and possessed 30,000 beeves and other flocks and herds innumerable. He was suspected of treason by Lord Essex, the deputy, though outwardly they remained friends. Sir Bryan MacPhelim O'Neill gave a feast, to which the Lord Justice and the chiefs of his people were invited, and they passed three days and nights together pleasantly and cheerfully. At the expiration of this time, as they were agreeably drinking and making merry, Sir Bryan, his brother, and his wife were seized upon by the Earl of Essex, and all his people put to the sword-men, women, and youths-in Sir Bryan's presence. Sir Bryan and his wife and brother were sent to Dublin, where they were tried and executed.

It was in the days of his successor, Con O'Neill, that the vast estates of this old princely family passed from it. Con O'Neill got into trouble, and was likely to lose his head. He was holding high state in his castle with his brothers, cousins, and relatives; wine ran short, and he sent his servants to Belfast, then a hamlet, for more, but they came back without it. Con was angry; a fight took place, and an English soldier was killed. Con was thrown into Carrickfergus Castle, the strongest fort in Ulster. Sir Arthur Chichester, who was then the English Deputy, proposed to hang him. Lady Con, however, found a friend willing to help her. This was Hugh Montgomery, sprung from the noble house of Eglinton, and destined to play a great part in the history of the neighbourhood of Belfast. He arranged for Con's rescue from Carrickfergus; so he escaped, and then Con agreed to cede half his lands in Clanaboye to Montgomery on condition that the latter obtained a free pardon from King James for him. Montgomery had recourse to his brother at court, who got the help of another Scot, James Hamilton, who in turn succeeded in getting Con's pardon from the King. Con's lands, however, had to satisfy James Hamilton as well as Hugh Montgomery. On April 16, 1605, letters patent were issued by the great seal "on the humble petition of Con M'Neal M'Bryan Fearlagh O'Neill, and of Hugh Montgomery, Esq., and James Hamilton, Esq., granting to the said James Hamilton all the lands in Upper Clanaboye and the Great Ards, which had been possessed by Con, or by his father, Bryan Fearlagh O'Neill in his lifetime." The northern half of County Down was handed over to Hamilton, who became bound to plant the land with English and Scottish blood over this great tract. James Hamilton became first Sir James and then Viscount Clanaboye, a title borne by his descendant, Lord Dufferin and Clanaboye. Montgomery became Lord Montgomery of the Ards, and, though the title is extinct, the Montgomerys still hold a portion of the land they then acquired, and still bury among the romantic ruins of Grey Abbey. Con soon ran through the remainder of his property and disappears from history, but his son fought for Charles I, and went into exile with Charles II.

James Hamilton

Hamilton and Montgomery were strong men, and did much for Ulster. Hamilton founded the towns of Bangor and Killyleagh, in County Down, and attended, too, to spiritual things, for he built churches in each of the six parishes embraced in his estate-Bangor, Killinchy, Holywood, Ballyhalbert, Dundonald, and Killyleagh. He made it his business to bring learned and pious ministers from Scotland, and planted all the parishes of his estate. To Hamilton fell the western portion of North Down, and to Montgomery the eastern. Montgomery also planted his estate, the country round Newtown and Donaghadee, known as the Great Ards. He was helped by his kinsman, Thomas Montgomery. The Montgomerys, Calderwoods, Agnews, Adairs, Cunninghams, and Shaws came to settle on the land in 1606, and built cottages and booths of sods and saplings, broke up the ground, and planted crops. The harvests of 1606 and 1607 were plentiful. The town of

Hugh Montgomery

Newtown - now Newtownards - grew up. Its ruined church was rebuilt by Sir Hugh Montgomery; the foundations of the industries of Ulster were also laid by him. Water-mills sprang up; spinning, too, was encouraged, and the success of this settlement made by Hamilton and Montgomery was complete. Four years after the foundation of the colony, Montgomery alone was able to bring before the King's Muster-Master one thousand able-bodied fighting-men to serve, when, out of them, a militia should be raised. This is how the vast estates of the Clanaboye O'Neills passed into the hands of the Scots, who have lived and flourished there ever since.

This branch of the O'Neill family was intimately connected with Belfast. Their principal stronghold was the grey castle of Castlereagh, once called " the Eagle's Nest." from its situation and the powerful influence of Con O'Neill. The coronation chair of the O'Neills is now in the museum in College Square. It was found among the ruins of the old castle, and was brought to Belfast in the year 1755.

The Plantation of Ulster in 1610

On the 14th September, 1607,   a ship lay at anchor in the Swilly, off Rathmullen, and before nightfall she set sail for France. On board were the Earls of Tyrone and Tyrconnell, and other Ulster chieftains who had conspired against King James I, and, the conspiracy being discovered, were fleeing from Ireland. Six counties were in consequence escheated (forfeited) to the Crown-Donegal, Derry, Tyrone, Fermanagh, Cavan, and Armagh. Antrim and Down were already partially occupied with Scots. The six escheated counties contained in all two million acres. Of these a million and a half, consisting of bog, forest, and mountain, were restored to the Irish; the half million acres of fertile land were settled with families of Scotch and English origin.

At the flight of the Earls, the province, by all accounts, was a vast wilderness. It could not well be otherwise after so many years of desolating strife. Soldiers and travellers tell us about the wild, inhospitable character of Ulster at the end of the sixteenth and beginning of the seventeenth centuries. In Shane O'Neill's time a report of the state of Ireland describes the county of Coleraine (which afterwards was made a portion of County Londonderry) as for the most part waste, and the neighbouring territory of Tyrone somewhat similar, having been reduced to such a state within a twelvemonth through quarrels among the O'Neills themselves.

"Woods and bog," "a very fast country full of wood and bog," are common descriptions as applied to the northern counties.

The policy of planting English colonies in Ireland was no new thing. Courtiers like the Earl of Essex and Sir Thomas Smith undertook the planting of colonies in Ulster, but with insufficient men and resources. It fell to a distinguished soldier of the late wars-Sir Arthur Chichester, a native of Devonshire, who had now been raised to the dignity of Lord Deputy of Ireland-to enter with masterly skill and statesmanship into the details of the projected Plantation. He had played a considerable part in the wars with the O'Neills. His qualities of head and heart were such as to entitle him to the high position he attained as head of the King's Irish Administration. Associated with him in the Government was another eminent man, Sir John Davies, the Attorney-General, whose fame as a writer and poet was enhanced by his letters on Irish affairs and his picturesque despatches and records of official movements.

Whoever his tutor may have been, Sir Arthur Chichester had got a firm grasp of the main principles that underlay and were to guide the Ulster settlement. An equality of estates that would not give excessive power to any person, but such as would induce men of influence to spend their fortunes on their lands, was of prime importance. His object was to foster a contented tenantry independent of the overlord, by giving them a potential interest in the improvement of their farms. This would directly hit the tribal custom, by which clansmen had no direct individual interest in the land. A second chief consideration with Sir Arthur Chichester was the native population. A contented native constituency was to his mind a necessary condition for a peaceful settlement.   While swordsmen and outlaws were to be got rid of, the position of the peasant with respect to his colonist neighbour merited careful attention. The general plan having been agreed upon, and approved by King James I, reports and conferences followed, which may be given in brief outline.

It was in the January of 1609 that "A Project for the division and plantation of the escheated lands in six several counties of Ulster, named Londonderry, Tyrone, Donegal, Fermanagh, Armagh, and Cavan," was issued. It contained a schedule of the lands to be divided, county by county, and definitely stated the scheme of allotment to the undertakers, the servitors, and the Church. Chief-Justice Ley and the Attorney-General Davies conferred with the King and Council with the result that the "orders and conditions to be observed by the undertakers" were published in March, 1609, the conditions being pretty much on the lines of those set forth in the "Project," but without the geographical particulars of the early document. The largest division of land, corresponding somewhat to a barony, was styled a "precinct," which was sub-divided into "proportions" of three sizes. The "great proportion" contained 2,000 acres; the "middle," 1,500 acres; and the "small," 1,000 acres. The provisions for building and for making freeholders and leaseholders, with other details of the organization of the settlements, completed the scheme.

By August, 1610, the lands were ready for occupation by the settlers, and a proclamation was issued with certain stipulations. Servitors and natives were to have freedom from rent for four years. They were to erect within three years upon a proportion of 1,000 acres one house of stone or brick with a bawn about it; and on a proportion of 1,000 acres merely a bawn or courtyard. These two classes also held their lands by the most favourable tenure-namely, a leasehold with a fixed rent; whereas the rest of the undertakers were to hold by a feudal tenure of Knight's service: which meant that they were to provide the Crown with a military force and arms. No mention, it will be observed, is made of the counties of Down and Antrim among the escheated territories. They had already been planted for the most part. The MacDonnells had received the larger part of County Antrim. In Down great and successful colonies were established by the Hamiltons and Montgomerys. Such is an outline of the settlement, but the work to be done by the settlers was both difficult and dangerous. When the walls of Jerusalem were being rebuilt after the captivity, Nehemiah tells us how the half of his servants wrought in the work, and the other half of them held both the spears and the habergeons.

In the Plantation days the new settlers met with difficulties not very different from those experienced by Nehemiah. Mr. George Canning, of Garvagh, the first agent of the Mercers' Company, tells us in his correspondence a pitiful tale of his dangers and troubles from pirates at the mouth of the river and robbers in the woods. To cope with the latter it was necessary to travel in companies well protected with arms, "Please send two pairs of bullet moulds and lead" was a significant request; yet, in spite of every difficulty, the intrepid settlers persevered in their work. Towns, villages, churches, and mills sprang up. They established trade and manufactures, en- closed fields, raised farmhouses and homesteads where there had been but robbers and their castles. Then for the first time the natural wealth of the country began to reveal itself. Commerce sprang up; busy fingers set to work on looms and spinning wheels; fields fenced and drained grew yellow corn, and vast flocks and herds were turned to profitable account. A live cattle trade was established with Bristol. The earth-tillers, formerly despised, were now encouraged. In 1580 the population was roughly half a million; in 1641 the population had risen to almost a million and a half. Ulster continued steadily to improve until the deplorable tragedy of 1641 so sadly reduced their numbers and retarded the progress of the Province for years.

THE RISING OF 1641 AND TRAGEDY OF THE ULSTER SETTLERS

"A PLAGUE on the Book! it has bred all this quarrel." This exclamation accompanied the insulting treatment meted out to a copy of the Bible in County Fermanagh at the outbreak of the rebellion of 1641. It was to be a religious war, but it was still more to be a war against the new settlers. It is admitted the country was prosperous and quiet, but the prosperity, it has been argued, was confined to the people of British extraction. To the chiefs who were dispossessed at the Plantation the English were piratical and heretic invaders, who were robbing them of their lands, liberties, and faith. It mattered little to the O'Neills and Maguires who was King of England. They desired to be quit of England. A report of the state of Ulster about 1630 represents the country as being sparsely inhabited, the "proportions" being wide and large; "for the Irish, of whom many townships might be formed, do not dwell together in any form, but wander with their cattle all the summer on the mountains, and all the winter in the woods; and until these Irish are settled, the English dare not live in those parts, for there is no safety either for their goods or lives, which is the main cause, though other reasons may be given, why they do not plentifully go thither and cheerfully plant themselves in the Province."

There existed thus in Ulster the very elements to produce the conflagration that soon came about. In his "Lays of the Western Gael" Sir Samuel Ferguson makes a pathetic lament for the native Irish:-

For the plain must be broke
By the share of the stranger,
And the stonemason's stroke
Tells the woods are in danger;
The green hills and shore
Be with white keeps disfigured,
And the Mote of Rathmore
Be the Saxon churl's haggard.

A new generation of settlers was springing up; the strong men of 1610, who, by their zeal and toil, had laid the foundations of Ulster's prosperity, were growing old when the rebellion broke out. On the morning of the 23rd of October, 1641, there appeared before the houses of the settlers and their tenants in the six escheated counties gangs of armed Irish, who demanded instant possession, and, being admitted, ejected the entire families and stripped them to the skin. Lord Wentworth had deprived the Presbyterian settlers of their arms, so they were comparatively helpless, yet many resisted and were killed. Vigorous young men sought shelter for their women and little ones in the houses of their Irish neighbours: the doors were opened, but within there dwelt not human beings but ferocious beasts. They were murdered, these helpless ones, with few exceptions. "Nakedness and famine" says Colonel Mervyn, "were judged over-slow executioners." Then entered the sword.

The rebels, under pretence of convoy, invited scattered and hidden settlers into a body, and the whole line, one by one, was exterminated. Sir William Cole saved Enniskillen. Naked men flying for their lives carried the alarm to Derry, Coleraine, and Carrickfergus, and the inhabitants had time to close their gates.

Charlemont Castle, the strongest fortress in Ulster, was surprised on the 23rd of October by Sir Phelim O'Neill, the leader of the rebels. Lord Caulfield, who was taken there, was afterwards murdered. In a fortnight every town, village, fort, or private house of a Protestant settler in the six counties, and in Down and Monaghan, were in the hands of the insurgents. Derry, Coleraine, and Enniskillen escaped.

The roads were covered with bands of miserable fugitives, flying to Dublin, Derry, or Carrickfergus. Murder, says Froude, was in the air. Savage creatures of both sexes yelping in chorus and brandishing their skenes; boys practising their young hands in stabbing and torturing English children: these were the scenes experienced through all Ulster. Farm stock, sheep, and men were slaughtered. If some found a few rags to cover them, they were torn away; if others, in modesty, twisted straw ropes round their waists, the straw was set on fire. Some were driven into the rivers and drowned. At least 80 of both sexes were thrown into the Bann from the bridge of Portadown; and for long years after, when the wind whistled on stormy nights, the ghosts of the slain were said to cry for revenge. Two cases are told of houses crowded with English and Scotch fugitives being burned down, and nearly all within reduced to ashes. Some were hanged, some mutilated, some ripped with knives. They put out grown men's eyes, and turned them adrift to wander and starve to death. Two cowboys boasted of having murdered thirty women and children. The insurgents in their madness swore they would not leave one English man, woman, or child alive. Coleraine suffered severely, being crowded with refugees. A pestilential fever broke out, and carried off thousands in several of the principal towns of County Antrim.

The number who lost their lives is uncertain. Sir John Temple estimated that 150,000 perished in two months; Clarendon, on cooler reflection, reduced the number to 40,000. A moderate and possible estimate was made by a gentleman who was forced with his wife to abandon his house, estate, and country, and arrived in London on the 15th of January, 1642. This writer says: "They have murdered and starved to death of the English in the Province of Ulster, and other Provinces, of men, women, and children, 20,000. They have stripped ladies and gentlewomen, virgins and babes, old and young, naked as ever they were born, turning them into the open fields. Many hundreds have been found dead in ditches with cold and want of food and raiment."

A truce was signed in September, 1643, between the king and the confederate insurgents. Later on both rebel and royalist sank alike under the avenging sword of Cromwell. The sieges of Drogheda and Wexford deserve to rank in horror with the most atrocious exploits of Tilly and Wallenstein, and made the name of Cromwell eternally hated in Ireland. The fall of these two towns virtually ended the war. Rebellion was played out, and they had to choose between submission and death. The remnant of the Ulster rebel leaders who had survived the wars were brought to justice. In 1652 a High Court of Justice under General Fleetwood was held at Kilkenny in the Hall of Assembly, to try them. Sir Phelim O'Neill and 200 others were convicted, condemned to death, and executed. Long and sad is the toll of death in those eventful years. According to the calculation of Sir William Petty, out of a population of 1,460,000, fully 616,000 had in eleven years perished by the sword, by the plague, or by famine artificially produced- a third part of the population had been blotted out. Thus ended one of the saddest and most cruel episodes in Irish history. There seems to have been comparative peace for almost two generations, when the dogs of war were again let loose in 1689-a year memorable for the siege of Derry and the defence of Enniskillen; followed, later, by the battle of the Boyne.

ARMAGH

THE past importance of this ancient city is noticed by several early writers, who describe it as the chief city in Ireland, St. Fiech, who flourished in the sixth century, calls it the seat of empire; Giraldus Cambrensis-the metropolis. It is supposed to derive its name from its characteristic situation - Ard-macha, signifying "the high place or field" or the height of Macha, the queen who founded Emania, 300 B.C. St. Patrick resided in Armagh for nine years, and made it the Primatial city. He founded the cathedral in 445. It was burnt down three times, but was always rebuilt. He also founded, near his own house, the monastery of St. Peter and St. Paul for Canons Regular of the Order of St. Augustine. Attached to it was a school or college, which long continued one of the most celebrated seminaries in Europe, and from which many learned men, not only of the Irish nation, but from all parts of Christendom, were despatched to diffuse knowledge throughout Europe. It is said that seven thousand students congregated in it in the pursuit of learning at one period. The Annals of Ulster relate that at a synod held by Gelasius in 1162, it was decreed that no person should lecture publicly on theology except such as had studied at Armagh.

Armagh

The city was destroyed by accidental conflagrations in the years 670, 687, and 770, and also sustained considerable injury in the last-mentioned year by lightning. In subsequent periods it suffered severely and repeatedly from the Danes; but perhaps it suffered more severely still in 1641, when it fell into the hands of Sir Phelim O'Neill, who, on being soon after forced to evacuate it, set fire to the cathedral, and put to death many of the inhabitants.

In 1170 the Synod of Armagh passed a decree that redounds to the credit of our country. The Primate and the Bishops assembled said: "Freedom was God's best gift to man, and no man had a right to hold his fellow-men in bondage." And by their decision every slave in Ireland was set free. Ireland, in consequence, was the first country in the civilised world to set the example; and from the year 1170 no slave was kept in this country. It was not till 1832 that Wilberforce brought his Bill into the English Parliament to free British slaves, and this Bill became law in 1836.

The fair city of Armagh is an interesting one. It was here the great hall of "Craobh Ruadh" was built, where the order of knighthood was established. The Knights of the Red Branch were the finest body of men who ever lived in Ireland. King Alfred the Great wrote a poem in 683, which can be seen in the

British Museum. He was educated in the school at Newry, and visited Armagh before returning to England. He mentions the beauty of the great church built by St. Patrick. This is one of the verses, as it is translated by O'Donovan:-

I found in Armagh the splendid
Meekness, wisdom, circumspection,
Fasting in obedience to the Son of God,
Noble and prosperous sages.

Town life, it is said, was alien to Irish civilisation till the Normans came. Certainly the Gaels were mainly a rural race, like all the northern peoples, till the founding of towns began in the tenth and eleventh centuries. Nevertheless, they had towns from the age of St. Patrick onward. In Armagh there were seven churches; and the city was divided into the Rath, the Great Third, the Third of Massay, and the Third of the Saxons (Trian Sacsan), the quarter formerly frequented by English students. Around these sacred places, and protected by their walls, dwelt lay traders and hereditary craftsmen, who busied themselves with the gold and silver work which they carried to so high a level. King James II in his progress through the north to and from the siege of Derry, rested for a few days at Armagh, which he described as having been pillaged by the enemy, and very inconvenient both for himself and his suite. In 1690 Duke Schomberg took possession of it, and formed a depot of provisions there.

No important event occurred after the revolution until the year 1760, when the city furnished a well-appointed troop of cavalry to oppose Thurot at Carrickfergus. In 1778, on the apprehension of an invasion from France and of civil disturbance, several of the inhabitants again formed themselves into a voluntary company, and offered the command to the Earl of Charlemont, by whom, after some deliberation, it was accepted. It is chiefly indebted for its present high state of improvement to the attention bestowed on it by several Primates since the Reformation, especially by Primate Boulter, and still more so by Primate Robinson, all of whom have made it their place of residence. It was Primate Robinson who erected the library, the palace, the college, and many fine and useful buildings; his name is also associated with the observatory, museum, and astronomical instruments. The present Royal School of Armagh, founded by King Charles I, in 1627, still keeps up the old traditions of learning and culture for which the city is famous.

Some interesting mementoes of the learning and sanctity of the olden times are still preserved. "The Book of Armagh," a Latin manuscript of the New Testament, with memories of St. Patrick, written in the year 807, is in the library of Trinity College, Dublin. "The Bell of Armagh," which is believed to have belonged to St. Patrick, is in the Royal Irish Academy. Bishop Reeves tells us that "no city is so rich in historical associations, and yet has so little to show and so little to tell in the present day." He says St. Patrick's first church is now represented by the Bank of Ireland; St. Peter and St. Paul's afford stabling and garden produce to a modern rus in urbe, and St. Mark's is lost in a dwelling-house. Enough, however, still remains to make the Primatial city a place full of memories, and a place to be proud of. As the ecclesiastical metropolis of both the Anglican and Roman organisations, it possesses two cathedrals -of which the Roman Catholic is of the more recent construction-and two archiepiscopal palaces. As the county town it has a courthouse, a prison, and a lunatic asylum. Almost all the buildings are built of limestone of the district, but the Anglican cathedral is of red sandstone.

DOWNPATRICK

DOWNPATRICK, which was anciently the residence of the native Irish Kings of Ulidia, was originally named Aras-Celtair and Rath-Keltair-one signifying the house, and the other the castle or fortification of Celtair, the son of Duach. Its present name is derived from its situation on a hill, and from its having been the chosen residence of St. Patrick, who, on his arrival there in 432, founded in its vicinity the abbey of Saul, and, shortly after, an abbey of regular canons near the ancient dun or fort, the site of which was granted to him by Dichu, son of Trichem, lord of the country, whom he had converted to the Christian faith. St. Patrick presided over these religious establishments till his death in 493.

A picturesque feature of the ancient Irish Church was that it was tribal in character. Around the church were grouped the houses, or rather the cells, of the bishops and other ecclesiastics belonging to the church. These cells in early days were mostly built of wattles, to be replaced in later times by circular stone houses, or "bee-hives," as they are generally called. Remains of these "bee-hives" are still to be seen in several parts of Ireland. The entire was enclosed by a circumvallation, called a "cashel," traces of which are still to be seen in the fields to the west of the cathedral.

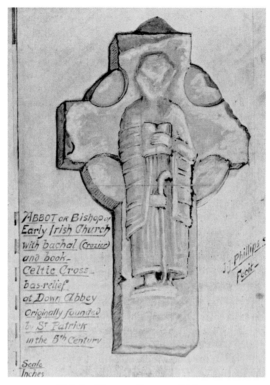

Celtic Cross, Down Abbey.

For more than six centuries after its foundation very little is known of the history of the cathedral. From what is recorded in various annals, we can see the wooden edifice founded and erected by St, Patrick not only as a religious establishment, but also as one of the many seats of learning for which Ireland was famed for centuries after the establishment of Christianity therein. St. Columba, or Columbkille, a native of County Donegal, received the greater part of his education at the neighbouring monastery of Movilla, under the tuition of St. Finnen. In 546 he founded the monastery at what is now the city of Derry. It is interesting here to note that the relics of St. Patrick had been enshrined by Columbkille, as is recorded in

"The Annals of Ulster":- The relics of St. Patrick were placed in a shrine at the end of three-score years after Patrick's death by Columbkille. Three splendid relics were found in the tomb; to wit -his goblet, the angels' gospel, and the bell of the

Testament. This is how the angel distributed the treasures for Columbkille - namely: the goblet to Down, the bell of the Testament to Armagh, and the angels' gospel to Columbkille himself.

In addition to the relics of St. Patrick, there were at that time in Downpatrick the relics of St. Brigid, the founder of the church of Kildare. "The Annals of the Four Masters" record her death, under the year 525, as follows: "On the first of February St. Brigid died, and was interred in Down in the same tomb with St. Patrick, with great honour and veneration." Tradition and history inform us that St. Columba also lies here, and that this distich in old monkish verse was written over them:-

Hi tres in Duno, tumulo tumulantur in uno
Brigida, Patricius, atque Columba pius.
(One tomb three saints contains, one vault below
Does Brigid, Patrick, and Columba shew.)

One of the knights who came to Dublin with the English invaders was John De Courcy. Seeing the extensive estates which his companions had gained in other parts of Ireland, he determined to try his fortune in Ulster, which had not yet been invaded. Having selected 22 knights and 200 soldiers, he set out from Dublin in the month of January, 1177, and in four days arrived at Downpatrick. The utmost terror filled the inhabitants at the sight of these adventurers. Taken completely by surprise, the King of Ulster fled with his followers to Armagh to seek aid from the chiefs of the north-west and the Archbishop of Armagh. This gave De Courcy time to establish himself, and he hastily erected what is probably the finest example of an early Norman mote-and-bailey castle now remaining in Ireland. This remarkable fortress lies about a quarter of a mile north of the cathedral, and the same distance north-west of the present town.

Before De Courcy had completed his castle or fort, King Mac Dunlevy returned with a huge following, numbering, according to Giraldus, 10,000 men. In his company were the Primate, the Bishop of Down, and a host of clergy, bearing with them holy and priceless relics of the early Irish Church; but for fighting purposes the army was a mere undisciplined rabble. They knew not the use of the bow and arrow, Giraldus tells us, and a glance at the huge fortification held by De Courcy shows how futile must have been their efforts to dislodge him. The Irish were utterly defeated, and all the clergy, with their precious relics, taken by the English. The bishops were afterwards set at liberty, and allowed to retain the Bell of St. Patrick and the Book of Armagh; but all the minor clergy were slain, and the rest of the holy relics kept by the English.

Downpatrick Cathedral

Thus were lost to the Irish Church many of its most sacred treasures. The Book of Armagh and the Bell of St. Patrick are still preserved to us, but all the other priceless relics carried to Down are lost for ever. De Courcy lived in almost royal state at Downpatrick, became the first Earl of Ulster, and subdued the greater part of the district known as Ulidia. He endowed the cathedral; it was much enlarged and beautified by him and Malachy. To them were also due the monastic buildings which were built, but of which there is not now a trace visible. They were erected prior to the visit of King John to Downpatrick in 1210. Edward Bruce plundered and burned the cathedral and part of the town in 1315, and repeated his visits in 1316 and 1318. On the latter occasion he caused himself to be proclaimed King of Ireland, but he was slain a few months later near Drogheda.

The cathedral, however, was rebuilt, only to be again totally demolished by the English, under Lord Deputy Grey, in 1538. It lay, a venerable ruin, for 250 years, until in 1790 a movement was made, chiefly by the county families of Down, to restore it. Dean W. Annesley took the initiative in 1789, and gave £300 a year of his income to help in the work. The Earl of Hillsborough, afterwards the first Marquis of Downshire, helped with a large subscription, and got King George II to give £1,000. It was not ready for service till 1818, and the west tower was not completed for some years after that date. Owing to the exertions of Dean Knox, who succeeded Dean Annesley, and Bishop Mant, the tower at the west end was finally completed.

The present name, Downpatrick, originates from a decree of John De Courcy, Earl of Ulster, who, to placate the Irish, gave it the name of Dun Patrick, or, as it is now called, Downpatrick. An interesting description of the town as it appeared in 1757 is given by one who wrote about it at that date: "The town is of considerable compass, and composed of four long streets centering near a point, not to mention lanes and other streets. It is distinguished into several quarters-as the Irish quarter, the English quarter, the Scotch quarter. Besides the benefits of markets and fairs, it has the advantage of being a borough town, and the electors are called 'pot-wallopers,' that is, all Protestants who boil a pot in the town, and pay Scot and Lot; and the seneschal of the manor is the returning officer. It was made the seat of a bishopric by St. Patrick; and the chapter of the cathedral as it now stands (1757) was constituted by letters patent of the seventh year of James I, consisting of six members. The bishopric has been united to the See of Connor since the year 1442."

BELFAST

IT is not to Belfast, the capital of the Northern State -the seat of government-the great commercial city of world-wide fame, but to Belfast and its environs in earlier days that the writer would refer. Belfast derives its name from the Irish words, "Beal Fearsad," or the mouth of the ford, there being in earlier times a ford near the situation of the present Queen's Bridge. It is built on an alluvial flat, and although at a very few feet above the level of the sea, it is considered to be a healthy city. Lying close to the mountains, its streets, which open in long vistas towards the hills, act as funnels to admit a constant current of pure mountain air into the very heart of the city.

As a city, Belfast has no ancient history. The ford, the castle, and the church were the three distinguishing objects that made the locality known in early days. The territory in which these places were situated was called in more remote times Dalaradia. Dalriada was the undisputed name of the territory in which the modern Belfast is situated. The distinction between it and Dalriada is clearly proved by Bishop Reeves in his "Ecclesiastical Antiquities of Down and Connor". He says:

(Dalriada, in the interior of County Antrim, never came as far as Ballymena, nor along the coast beyond Larne - it was the northern half of the county, and the name, contractedly written Ruta, is still called the Route; but Dalaradia stretched, in the most extended meaning, from Newry in the County Down to the mountain Slemlsh in the County of Antrim, including in that wide scope the site of Belfast."

The lough or bay of Belfast was known as Loch Laoigh, or as Lacus Vituli, according to Adamnan, and was the frequent resort of the roving Danes in the early centuries of our era. The Norman knight, John De Courcy, created Earl of Ulster by Henry II, who lived in almost regal splendour at Downpatrick, and was called by the monkish chronicler "Prince of Ulidia," embracing the two counties of Down and Antrim, is supposed to have built the first castle of Belfast close to the ford of the river. He was the first Anglo-Norman or English possessor of the site of Belfast and the surrounding country. At an early period an open river ran down the centre of High Street, which was crossed by six bridges. Small thatched houses occupied the ground at each side of the river. The three principal buildings in the town were the castle, where Castle Place is now; the market house, at the corner of High Street and Corn Market; and the church or chapel of the ford, where St. George's Church now stands.

The first church of which we have any record was called the Church of St. Patrick of the White Ford; later on it was known as Shankill, or the old church. It was a place of importance, for it had six altarages or small churches attached to it. There is not a vestige left now of the church, and an unsightly mound marks the spot where it once stood. The old graveyard is still very occasionally used by families who possess a right to bury there. The nearest church to Shankill was mentioned in 1306 as being one of the "altarages". It was the chapel of "The Ford," afterwards known as the "Corporation Church." This was the church to which the Sovereign, or Mayor, and the Town Council went in state on Sundays. We know it now as St. George's Church, in High Street. The old chapel of the ford was a small building close to the river. It was largely used by travellers, who entered the church to offer prayers for their safe journey before they attempted the dangerous crossing of the River Lagan, for it was a very hazardous undertaking in those days. Both of these buildings were standing in 1306, and probably long before that remote period.

For more than one hundred years the Anglo-Normans increased and consolidated their forces in north-eastern Ulster. Castles were built, the sites of many of which are yet known, and improvements spread all over the country; but this consolidation received a rude shock from the invasion of Edward Bruce in 1315, who laid waste Belfast, Greencastle, Newtown, and many other towns. In the reign of Queen Elizabeth the town and fortress fell into the hands of Sir Thomas Smyth, a favourite of the Queen; but were afterwards given to Lord Essex, and then, in the reign of King James I, to the Lord Deputy, Sir Arthur Chichester, who in 1612 was created Baron Chichester. At this time the town consisted of about 120 houses, mostly built of mud and covered with thatch. The old castle, too, was in a tumbledown condition. Sir Arthur built a great house, and let his lands on long leases, largely to the officers of his army, so that they might do their duty to him.

The survey of 1611 tells us how the settlement was progressing. What is now covered by southern Belfast had been leased for 61 years at £10 per annum to Moses Hill, sometime lieutenant of his troop of horse. From this Moses Hill is descended the Marquis of Downshire. Hill was busy building a new castle on the site of the old ruin of De Courcy's castle. It was surrounded by spacious gardens. It is curious to read of hunting, hawking, and other sports, in the woods and meadows where now are long streets of houses.

King William III was received here in 1690. He admired the castle, pleasure grounds, and gardens so much that he remained on a visit of five days. There were only two places of worship in the town at that time; the old Corporation Church in High

High Street, Belfast in the 16th century.

(From watercolour drawing in the M'Cowan Collection, Belfast Municipal Museum.

Street and the Presbyterian meeting-house in Rosemary Lane - the Roman Catholics not being permitted to build their chapels within the walls of corporate towns. In 1769 the castle gardens and the castle meadows were still in all their luxuriance. The gardens reached to the waterside, and the meadows extended over a great tract of ground now occupied by some of the finest buildings and streets which the city contains. Donegall Place, Donegall Square, and other streets adjoining were gardens or meadows, with shady walks and pleasant groves, and the water approached so nearly to the southern side that it was stated some years since by an old person who was witness of the fact, that Lord Donegall's pleasure boat was moored about the present Arthur Street. The ruins of the Castle of Belfast adjoining Donegall Place were remembered by an old inhabitant, now no longer alive.

During the civil commotions which so long afflicted the country Belfast suffered less than most places, and it soon after attained the rank of the "greatest town for trade in the North of Ireland." James Blow introduced letterpress printing in 1696, and in 1704 issued the first copy of the Bible produced in the island. In September, 1737, Henry and Robert Joy started the "Belfast News-Letter." Twenty years afterwards the town contained 1,800 houses and 8,549 inhabitants.

It was not, however, till 1789 that Belfast obtained the regular communication which towns of less importance already enjoyed with Dublin by stage coach, a fact which is to be explained by the badness of the roads and the steepness of the hills between Newry and Belfast. Belfast Lough is exceedingly picturesque, whether entered by the Antrim or by the Down side of the channel. The outer harbour is one of the safest in the kingdom. Great improvements were made about seventy years ago on the more immediate entrance to the port. The course of the Lagan, which runs past the quays down to Garmoyle, was originally most tortuous and somewhat difficult to navigate, but about 1840 the late William Dargan was employed to make a straight cut from the lower part of the harbour, and to deepen the channel so that ships of large draughts can be brought to the quays, which extend for about a mile below Queen's Bridge.

From such small beginnings-through the industry, grit and perseverance of her citizens-the city of Belfast has become today one of the first commercial cities of the Empire, and the capital of Northern Ireland.

Origin of the Ulster Linen Trade and Shipbuilding

MANY have been the immigrants to Ireland at various periods of her history, but none have had more important results than the immigration of the French Huguenots, which took place at the close of the seventeenth and beginning of the eighteenth centuries. For a long time the Huguenots enjoyed toleration in France under the celebrated "Edict of Nantes"; but on Thursday, the 8th of October, 1685, the fatal edict revoking the "Edict of Nantes" was signed, and the doom of the Protestant Church in that country was sealed. Those who could hastened to the frontiers, but these were strongly guarded, as Louis XIV did not wish to lose such good subjects. However, by gaining over some of the guards, no fewer than 50,000 families were enabled to escape. Those who passed into Holland at once received patronage and protection from William, Prince of Orange, and all who had served in the French army received commissions of equal rank in his service, and accompanied him to England and, eventually, to Ireland.

Here, after peace was restored, they formed several settlements. The chief localities of the colonies in Ireland were Lisburn (then called Lisnagarvey), Dundalk, Dublin, Portarlington, Youghal, and Cork. Here they enjoyed many

Louis Crommelin

religious privileges, having their own pastors, their services in their own language, and their ministers supported by the State. In Portarlington the service was performed in the French language till the early part of the eighteenth century.

An article written some seventy years ago describes the Huguenot settlement in Lisburn. This settlement owes its prosperity to the fact that the Government of that day was desirous of discouraging the woollen manufacture in Ireland, as injurious to England, and of encouraging the linen manufacture in its stead. To foster the linen trade King William III invited over from Holland Louis Crommelin, a French Huguenot who had obtained great celebrity in the linen trade in that country, and who was considered the most suitable person to introduce the manufacture, in its most improved state, into Ireland. Accordingly, in 1698, he left Holland, accompanied by his son, and proceeded to the North of Ireland to examine what place would be best adapted for the undertaking. After due consideration he selected Lisnagarvey, in the County of Down, as the centre of the proposed settlement. The King, who took great interest in the project, approved of the site, and appointed Louis Crommelin overseer of the Royal Linen Manufacture of Ireland. He encouraged him to invite others over, both of high and low rank, to take part in establishing the manufacture and instructing the natives, promising to befriend all who came, and granting a premium of £5 for every room kept going. Louis Crommelin brought over from Holland 1,000 looms and spinning-wheels of an improved construction, and invited a number of French and other families, mostly Huguenots like himself, who gladly complied, and soon founded quite a colony among themselves. Three of these were appointed assistants to Louis at a yearly salary of £120 each. A church was built for the accommodation of the community, and a chaplain ordained, receiving £60 a year. Their original Bible and Prayer Book in the French language are still preserved. This colony consisted, besides the Crommelins, of about twenty-seven families, who were accompanied by many respectable tradesmen. These settlers closely adhered to each other, generally intermarrying for two or three generations.

King William III, after some time, considering that Louis Crommelin had expended out of his private fortune £10,000 of capital on the undertaking, granted him a pension of, £200 a year during his life. Louis asked it to be given to his son, which was done, but he soon died, and the pension reverted to the Crown. Louis Crommelin had many personal interviews with the King, who showed him much favour; and he likewise received the formal thanks of the Irish Parliament in 1707. He was followed to Ireland sometime after by two of his brothers, who brought with them a capital of £20,000, they having been left £10,000 each by their father. Several tradesmen came with them. Closely connected with the Crommelin family was that of De Lacherois, also Huguenot refugees, and forming part of the colony of Lisburn. A Nicholas Delacherois and his brother were officers in the army of King William III, and in 1689, when King William first came over to Ireland accompanied by his

French guards, the two brothers distinguished themselves at the battle of the Boyne. Lisnagarvey had, at the time of Louis Crommelin, recovered from the siege of the Irish rebels under Sir Phelim O'Neill. There were not more than one hundred tenements, besides the castle, then remaining perfect. The town returned two members to the Irish Parliament, and was the residence of the Bishop of the united diocese of Down and Connor, its church being the cathedral of the diocese. A wooden bridge here crossed the Lagan, and it was at the foot of this bridge, at the western side of Bridge Street, that Louis Crommelin built the first linen factory, the old watercourse of which remained until the beginning of the nineteenth century. He also established a bleach-green in the vicinity. It is known, says the writer from whom I have quoted, that linen was manufactured in Ireland from the earliest ages, and it is said by some to have been introduced (with the spindle and loom) by the Phœnicians, but, of course, in a comparatively imperfect state; yet it was extensively used, and formed even a considerable article of commerce, as is proved by an Act of Henry VIII, and another restricting the higher orders from wearing an extravagant quantity of linen in their shirts. It was exported as early as the reign of Henry III. The Irish people used it largely in their garments, the long "cota" being made of it, as Camden mentions that O'Neill and his followers were so clad when they visited Queen Elizabeth. Such is the story of the early history of the linen industry of Ulster - an industry which, since those days, has steadily increased, and, together with the shipbuilding trade, has made the fame of Ulster resound through the world. As to the shipbuilding trade, it was a fortunate chance that brought the industry to Belfast. A modern writer describes how Edward Harland, a young Englishman whose training had been in the shipyards, came to Ireland in search of a convenient site for shipbuilding. He tried Dublin, where the Dublin Port and Docks Board - a conservative body - turned his proposals down. He went to Belfast, and, for the sum of £500, bought a suitable pitch whereon to start his little works. They were, indeed, small; the visitor to-day can see an entry in the books of Harland and Wolff-Wolff was a Dutchman who joined in the venture-" Advanced Edward Harland thirty shillings. "This was the germ of one of the greatest shipbuilding industries in the world, whose wages bill eventually reached £50,000 a week. There were no strikes. The Belfast working-man is an uncommonly good workman, with intelligence enough to see on which side his bread is buttered. The shipyard, or rather shipyards-for the ordinary process followed, that one successful industry begat another of the same kind-employed the men; the linen industry the women. The combination is the secret of Belfast's amazing progress. Capital accumulated; and it was capital not of the dormant but of the active, creative type. It flowed into all sorts of channels, and fed all kinds of industries-tobacco manufacturers, ropeworks, and the like. Hard work and enterprise brought success.

ANTRIM

THE town of Antrim, in the county of Antrim, is some thirteen miles from Belfast. This place was anciently called Entruim, Entrummia, or Entrum Neagh, signifying, according to some writers, "the habitation upon the waters," probably from its contiguity to Lough Neagh. The earliest notice of it occurs in the year 495, Mr, Lewis tells us, when Aodh, a disciple of St. Patrick, founded a monastery there, which was destroyed during the Danish incursions, and of which no further mention appears till the foundation of Woodburn Abbey, to which it became an appendage. A sanguinary battle between the native Irish and the English took place near the town, when Sir Robert Savage, one of the earliest English settlers, is said, with a small part of his forces, to have killed more than 3,000 of the Irish army.

In the thirteenth year of King James I the town and sixteen townlands of the parish, together with the advowson of the living and the rectorial tithes, were granted to Sir Arthur Chichester. In 1643 a naval engagement took place on Lough Neagh, when Colonel Conolly and Captain Longford gave battle to a party of Irish marauders, who at that time had possession of the fort of Charlemont, near the shore of Clanbrassie, on which occasion the Irish were defeated and their

Round Tower, Antrim.

fleet brought by the victors in triumph to the town. In 1649 the town was burnt by General Munro; and in 1688 a party of Lord Blantyre's troops, being separated from the main body of the army, crossed the River Bann at Toome, and were made prisoners in a skirmish near this place. On 7th June, 1798, a rebellion broke out at Antrim, the rebels numbering from 3,000 to 4,000 men. Their leader was a young Belfast cotton manufacturer named Henry Joy M'Cracken, amiable and good. The Government had information. Colonel Lumley, with two or three troops of dragoons, two cannon, and a body of yeomanry, defended it. A sharp fight, lasting between two and three hours, took place in the streets of the town. The rebels endured several charges, and then retired to Lord Massereene's grounds. Colonel Lumley was wounded and Lord O'Neill was killed. The rebels were at last driven back, and between 200 and 400 were killed. They fled in all directions, leaving behind them about 3,000 pikes and muskets.

The town of Antrim is situated on the banks of the Sixmilewater river, on the great road from Belfast to Londonderry, and in one of the most fertile and beautiful valleys in the county; it consists of two principal streets, and others branching from them. The situation of the town, within a quarter of a mile of the north-eastern portion of Lough Neagh, where a small rude quay or pier has been constructed, is favourable to the increase of its trade, from the facility of water conveyance afforded by the lake, the Belfast canal, and the Upper Bann. Several patents granting fairs and markets are extant, of which the earliest, granting to Sir James Hamilton a market on Thursday, is dated February 14th, 1605. The church originally built in 1596 was destroyed by fire in 1649, and remained in ruins till 1720, when it was rebuilt; a lofty square embattled tower, surmounted by an elegant octagonal spire of freestone, was added in 1812. About half a mile to the north-east of the church, in a part of the valley leading to Lough Neagh, is one of the most perfect round towers in the island. It is built of unhewn stone and mortar, perfectly cylindrical in form, and is 95 feet in height, and 49 feet in circumference at the base; the summit terminates with a cone 12 feet high; the door is on the north side, and at a height of 7 feet 9 inches from the ground; the walls are 2 feet 9 inches in thickness; and the tower contains four storeys, the ascent to which appears to have been by a spiral staircase. Each of the three lower storeys is lighted by a square window, and the upper storey by four square perforations. Corresponding with the cardinal points, above the doorway is a Grecian cross, rudely sculptured in alto-relievo on a block of freestone, which appears to be part of the original building. Around the base of the tower great quantities of human bones and some vestiges of the foundations of buildings have been discovered. The latter are supposed to indicate the site of the ancient monastery founded by Aodh. In a garden adjoining the tower is a large detached mass of basalt, having nearly a level surface, in which are two cavities or basins,

Shane's Castle.

evidently the work of art, of which the larger is 19 inches in length, 16 inches wide, and 9 inches deep, and during the driest season is constantly filled with fine clear water.

Lough Neagh is close to the town. It is the largest lake in the British Isles, and is chiefly in County Antrim, but extends into several others. It is traditionally stated to have been formed in the year 62 by an irruption of the sea, but is obviously formed by the consilience of the Blackwater, Upper Bann, and four other rivers. The lake is about 20 English miles in length from N.E. to S.W., and about 12 miles in extreme breadth from east to west; 80 miles in circumference, and comprises about 154 square miles. Its greatest depth in the middle is 45 feet. According to the Ordnance Survey it is 48 feet above the level of the sea at low water. The only outlet is the Lower Bann. In some places the waters possess medicinal properties, which they are supposed to derive from the adjacent shore. They have also petrifying powers, but these are supposed to exist in the soil, as purifications are only found in the lake near the shore of County Antrim.

Sir Arthur Chichester in 1604 received from James I a grant of the fisheries, and of the office of Admiral of Lough Neagh, which have been held by his successors, and are now vested in the Marquis of Donegall. Inspired by the glories of days gone by, Thomas Moore, our Irish poet, writes:-

On Lough Neagh's banks as the fisherman strays,
When the clear cold eve's declining,
He sees the round towers of other days
In   the   waves beneath him shining.
Thus shall memory often, in dreams sublime,
Catch a glimpse of the days that are over;
Thus, sighing, look through the waves of time
For the long-faded glories they cover.

DERRY

To a stranger sailing up Lough Foyle to-day, the view of the Maiden City rising so majestically above its waters will long be a cherished memory. It is not easy to realise that a British officer sailing over the same waters in 1567 found nothing on the site of the present city but a deserted monastery of Augustine monks. Its fame in early times was chiefly ecclesiastical. In the "Annals of the Four Masters" it is called Derry Columbkill, after St. Columb, who built a monastery here in A.D. 546, and who, from the number of churches he built, obtained the addition to his name of "ceille" or "kill"- that is, of the "cells" or "churches." The ancient name of Derry was Daire Calgac, which signifies the oaks of Calgac, or the territory of oaks pertaining to Calgac. Ireland was in those days the genuine country of the oak, and so we have many places called by the oaks; as Derry-ar, Derry-lane, Derry-beg, Derry-more. So abundant was the oak timber in our island in former times, that it was exported to the continent for shipbuilding and many other purposes, and we have it on good testimony that Westminster Abbey is at this day roofed with our Irish glen-wood oak. The glen-wood or coppice, where the best oak was produced, lay in the south-eastern parts of the County Derry, from Maghera to beyond Bellaghy and Magherafelt, and near Desertmartin, the so much celebrated royal oak claimed as a privilege by some of the Georges.

Derry

It was in 1567 that Colonel Randolph, an English officer was sent from Bristol to the aid of Sir Henry Sidney, the Deputy, to suppress the rebellion of Tyrone. He had a rough and stormy passage, and did not reach Lough Foyle for fourteen days. As he sailed up to Derry his keen eye was struck with the formation of the ground for defence, and he considered the site well suited to build a colony. Soon afterwards he fell in battle, and his men had a trying time. They had pitched their camp on the grounds of the old monastery, and the men were sleeping over the graves of the monks. Many were stricken with serious illness, and the death-roll was heavy. The troops were removed to healthier quarters, and, for a time, the plan of building a colony was deferred, but not forgotten. Years afterwards Queen Elizabeth wrote impatiently to Lord Essex: "How often have you resolved us that until Lough Foyle and Ballyshannon were planted there could be no hope of doing service to the rebels." This was, however, at length attained by Sir Henry Dockwra, with a force of 4,000 foot and 200 horse. On the 16th of April, 1600, he landed at Culmore, and six days after took Derry without opposition. Sir Henry thus describes the city: "A place in the manner of an island, comprehending within it 40 acres of land, whereon were the ruins of an old abbey, a bishop's house, two churches, and, at one of the ends of it, an old castle; the river called Lough Foyle encompassing it on one side, and a bog most commonly wet and not easily passable, except in two or three places, dividing it from the mainland." The following description of the first or original town will be of interest. Sir Henry Dockwra stated that he employed "the two ships of war with soldiers in them to coast all along the shore for twenty or thirty miles, and willed wheresoever they found any houses they should bring away the timber and other material to build withal; and O'Cane having a wood lying on the opposite side with plenty of grown birch, I daily sent some workmen with a guard to cut it down, and not a stick of it but was fought for. A quarry of stone and slate we found hard bye, cockle shells to make lyme we discovered infinite plentie in a little island at the mouth of the harbour. With these helps and the stones and rubbish of old buildings we found, we set ourselves wholie to fortifying and framing and setting up houses such as we might be able to live in." Dockwra's town of Derry was built in 1600, before the Plantation of Ulster. It had a short life. Eight years afterwards it was burned down by Sir Cahir O'Doherty, and its English Governor (Sir George Pawlet) and the garrison were put to the sword by the young chief of Inishowen.

Following the plantation of 1609, referred to in the opening chapter, we find that on the 29th of January, 1613, the Irish Society was formed, and received its charter in the March following, granting the city or town of Derry, with a circuit of three miles round from the centre of the town, to be a county in itself; the lands in the west of the Foyle, containing about 4,000 acres, besides bog and mountain, which were to be regarded as waste acres belonging to the city. The walls were required to be finished, and for this purpose a grant of £5,000 was made in 1615.

The whole barony of Loughinshollin, with the great woods thereon, was added to their territory. 4,000 acres were taken from Donegal and 8,000 from Antrim to form the liberties of Derry and Coleraine respectively, both towns being under the control of the Irish Society. The little county of Coleraine thus enlarged became the modern county of Londonderry. The total number of houses built from 1609 to 1629 to restore the ruined city of Derry, exclusive of the bishop's and dean's, was 110, the cost of which was £13,450; and, in addition, a sum of £14,000 had been expended for fortifications and other matters within the city.

In the Rising of 1641 it became an object of the insurgents to seize the city of Derry, but the plot was discovered, and Derry became the chief refuge for the English and Scotch settlers. The city was put into a state of defence. The twelve companies sent each two pieces of ordnance, which, with the twenty placed in a battery some years before, constituted a sufficient force to resist the fury of the rebels. Upon the termination of the rebellion commissioners were sent over to settle affairs and demise leases, renewing all the leases in Derry and Coleraine; and upon the restoration of Charles II letters patent were formally granted on 10th April, 1662, confirming the charter of James I in a full and explicit manner.

For some years there was comparative peace and quietness in the city, till 1688, when the great event occurred which has rendered the name of Derry famous in history. The siege furnishes one of the brightest instances of patriotic heroism that is to be found in the annals of any nation. A rumour spread over the whole island that on the 9th of December there would be a general massacre of the Protestant settlers. For some time there had been a large emigration of timid and quiet people from the Irish ports to England. Those who remained began in almost every county to draw close together. Every large country house became a fortress; every visitor who arrived after nightfall was challenged from a loophole or barricaded window, and if he attempted to enter without passwords and explanations a blunderbuss was presented at him.

On the dreaded night of December the 9th there was scarcely one Protestant mansion from the Giant's Causeway to Bantry Bay in which armed men were not watching and lights burning from the early sunset to the late sunrise. The people of Londonderry shared in this alarm, and soon news came that a regiment of 1,200 men, under the command of the Earl of Antrim, had received orders to occupy the city for King James, and was already on the march from Coleraine. The consternation was extreme. Some were for closing the gates and resisting, some for temporising. Lord Antrim was meanwhile drawing nearer and nearer. At length the citizens saw from the walls his troops arrayed on the opposite shore of the Foyle. There was no bridge at that time, but there was a ferry which kept up constant communication between the two banks of the river, and by this ferry a detachment from Lord Antrim's regiment crossed. The officers presented themselves at the gate, produced a warrant, and demanded admittance and quarters for King James's soldiers. Just at this moment thirteen young apprentices flew to the guardroom, themselves seized the keys of the city, rushed to the Ferryquay gate, closed it in the face of King James's officers, and let down the portcullis.

A great army in the service of King James was ordered to march northwards. As they advanced whole towns were left in ruins without one inhabitant. The people of Omagh destroyed their own dwellings so utterly that no roof was left to shelter the enemy from the rain and wind. The people of Lisburn fled to Antrim, and as the foes drew nearer all Lisburn and Antrim together came pouring into Londonderry. Thirty thousand Protestants of both sexes, and of every age, were crowded behind the bulwarks of the city of refuge. There, at length, on the verge of the ocean, hunted to the last asylum, the Imperial race turned desperately at bay.

King James himself had meanwhile sailed from Brest, and landed at Kinsale on the afternoon of the 12th of March. Soon after his arrival he hastened towards Londonderry, where his

Derry in 1688.

army was concentrated a few miles south of the city. The two French generals, Rosen and Maumont, who had sailed with him from Brest, were in his tram. Confident of success the King approached within 100 yards of the southern gate of the city, and was received with a shout of "No surrender."

King James retired to Dublin, accompanied by Rosen, the direction of the siege being entrusted to Maumont. The besiegers began by battering the town. It was soon on fire in several places, yet the spirits of the people rose so high that their chiefs thought it safe to act on the offensive. On 21st April a sally was made under the command of Colonel Murray. The Irish stood their ground resolutely, and a furious and bloody contest took place. Maumont, at the head of a body of cavalry, flew to the place where the fight was raging. He was struck on the head with a musket ball and was killed. The besiegers lost several other officers and about 200 men before the garrison could be driven in. Murray escaped with difficulty. His horse was killed under him, and he was beset by his enemies; but he was able to defend himself till some of his friends made a rush from the gate to his rescue, with Governor Walker at their head. In consequence of the death of Maumont, Richard Hamilton became commander of the Irish army. He was a fine gentleman and a brave soldier; but he had no pretensions to the character of a great general, and had never seen a siege. Pusignay had more science and energy, but he fell in battle a fortnight after Maumont.

It seemed that the siege must be turned into a blockade, but another determined effort was to be made first. The point selected for assault was an outwork called Windmill Hill, not far from the southern gate. Many volunteers bound themselves by oath to make their way into the works or perish in the attempt. Captain Butler, son of Lord Mountgarret, undertook to lead the sworn men to the attack. On the walls the besieged were drawn up in three ranks. The office of those who were behind was to load the muskets of those who were in front. The besiegers came on boldly, but after long and hard fighting were driven back. The women of Derry were seen amidst the thickest fire, serving out water and ammunition to their husbands and brothers. In one place, where the wall was only seven feet high, Captain Butler and some of his sworn men succeeded in reaching the top, but they were all killed or made prisoners. At length, after 400 had fallen, their chiefs ordered a retreat. Nothing was left but to try the effect of hunger. It was known that the stock of food in the city was slender. Every precaution was now taken by the besiegers against the introduction of provisions, all the avenues leading to the city by land being closely guarded. The river was fringed with forts and batteries, which no vessel could pass without great peril. After some time it was determined to make security still more complete by throwing a barricade across the stream about a mile and a half below the city. Several boats full of stones were sunk. A row of stakes was driven into the bed of the river. Large pieces of fir wood, strongly bound together, formed a boom which was more than a quarter of a mile in length, and which was firmly fastened to both shores by cables a foot thick.

The Walker Monument.

Within the walls of Derry the distress had become acute. So early as the 8th of June horseflesh was almost the only meat which could be procured, and the supply was scanty. It was necessary to make up the deficiency with tallow, and even tallow was doled out with a parsimonious hand. Pestilence made its appearance in the train of hunger; fifteen officers died of fever in one day, and among the number was the military governor, Baker.

By the end of July the fighting men of the garrison were so exhausted that they could scarcely keep their legs. Even in that extremity the general cry was "No surrender" and there were not wanting voices which in low tones added: "First the horses and hides, and then the prisoners, and then each other." At this crisis Captain Kirke, who with his fleet had remained inactive for some weeks in Lough Foyle, received positive orders that Derry must be relieved. He accordingly determined to make an attempt to do so. Among the merchant ships which came to Lough Foyle under his convoy was one called the "Mountjoy." The master, Michaiah Browning, a native of Londonderry, had brought from England a large cargo of provisions. He had, it is said, repeatedly remonstrated against the inaction of the armament. He now eagerly volunteered to take the first risk of succouring his fellow-citizens, and his offer was accepted. Andrew Douglas, master of the "Phœnix," who had on board a quantity of meal from Scotland, was willing to share the danger and the honour. The two merchantmen were to be escorted by the "Dartmouth" frigate of 36 guns, commanded by Captain John Leake, afterwards an admiral of great fame.

It was the 30th of July, the sun had just set, the evening sermon in the cathedral was over, the congregation had separated, when the sentinels on the tower saw the sails of three vessels coming up the Foyle. Soon there was a stir in the Irish camp. The besiegers were on the alert for miles along both shores. The ships were in extreme peril, for the river was low, and the only navigable channel ran very near to the left bank, where the headquarters of the enemy had been fixed, and where the batteries were most numerous.

At length the little squadron came to the place of peril; then the "Mountjoy" took the lead, and went right at the boom. The huge barricade cracked and gave way, but the shock was such that the "Mount joy" rebounded and stuck in the mud. A yell of triumph rose from the banks.

The besiegers rushed to the boats, and were preparing to board, but the "Dartmouth" poured on them a well directed broadside, which threw them into disorder. Just then the "Phœnix" dashed at the breach which the "Mountjoy" had made, and was in a moment within the fence. Meanwhile the tide was rising fast. The "Mount joy" began to move, and soon passed safely through the broken stakes of floating spars; but her brave master was no more; a shot from one of the batteries had struck him, and he died in sight of the city which was his

Londonderry in 1793.

birthplace, which was his home, and which had just been saved by his courage and self-sacrifice.

Even after the barricade had been passed, there was a terrible hour of suspense. It was ten o'clock before the ships arrived at the quay. The whole population was there to welcome them. A screen made of casks filled with earth was hastily thrown up to protect the landing-place from the batteries on the other side of the river, and then the work of unloading began. First were rolled on shore barrels containing 6,000 bushels of meal. Then came great cheeses, flitches of bacon, kegs of butter, sacks of peas and biscuit, ankers of brandy. Not many hours before half a pound of tallow and three-quarters of a pound of salted hide had been weighed out with niggardly care to every sighting man. The rations which each now received were three pounds of flour, two pounds of beef, and a pint of peas. The besiegers' guns continued to roar all night, and all night the bells of the rescued city made answer to the Irish guns with a peal of joyous defiance. Through the whole of the 31st of July the batteries of the enemy continued to play, but soon after the sun had again gone down flames were seen arising from the camp, and when the 1st of August dawned a line of smoking ruins marked the site lately occupied by the huts of the besiegers, and the citizens saw far off the long column of pikes and standards retreating up the left bank of the Foyle towards Strabane. The siege had lasted 105 days. The garrison had been reduced from about 7,000 effective men to about 3,000; and the loss of the besiegers, according to Governor Walker, was 8,000.

So ended the great siege of Derry, says Lord Macaulay, from whom I quote, the most memorable in the annals of the British Isles. Generations have passed since then; but today even Ulsterman, of whatever class or creed, may well look back with pride to the grit and endurance of his countrymen in the city of Derry in the spring and summer of 1689.

58

INISHOWEN

INISHOWEN, now under the government of the Irish Free State, has been the scene of many stirring events in the history of Ulster. The peninsula stretches twenty-two miles in length and sixteen and a half miles at its greatest breadth. The coast is bold and majestic, the surface mountainous and wild. Inishowen derives its name from Kinel Owen, one of the sons of Nial the Great, commonly called Nial of the Nine Hostages. In the commencement of the fifth century, when that monarch divided the greater part of Ireland between his twelve sons, this district was allotted to Eogan or Owen, who gave it the name of Inishowen, or the Island of Owen, from the fact of its being surrounded almost entirely by water, Lough Foyle, Lough Swilly, and the Atlantic Ocean enclosing it on all sides, except for a narrow neck of land about five miles across. The Macloughlins, the O'Deerys, the O'Gormleys, are ancient families descended from the branch of the northern Hy Niall. It was on Lough Swilly that a ship lay at anchor off Rathmullen on the 14th September, 1607, and before nightfall it had carried away, to use the language of the Four Masters, "a distinguished company of whom the sea has not borne and the wind has not wafted in modern times a number of persons in one ship more eminent, illustrious, or noble, in point of genealogy, heroic deeds, valour, feats of arms, and brave achievements than they." It was "The Flight of the Earls" from their native land, the great Ulster chieftains who so long resisted the power of England, and by their flight opened up the way for the Plantation of Ulster. One hundred and ninety years later a French squadron under Bompard and Hardy appeared in Lough Swilly. The squadron consisted of the "Hoche," a 74-gun ship, and eight frigates. On board the "Hoche" was Wolfe Tone. To avoid the English admiral, Sir John Warren, who was known to be on the watch for them, they made a long circuit into the Atlantic. They were separated in a storm, and on the 10th of October, 1798, the "Hoche" and three frigates found themselves alone at the mouth of Lough Swilly, with Warren, in pursuit of them, already in sight. The frigates, drawing little water, escaped. Wolfe Tone, says Froude, was entreated to fly with them, but chose to remain. The "Hoche" fought for six hours against four ships as large as herself, and did not strike till she was sinking. Wolfe Tone distinguished himself in action, and in his French uniform was not recognised. The defeated were invited to breakfast by Lord Cavan; Wolfe Tone accompanied the French officers, and was instantly arrested by Sir George Hill. He expected his commission in the French army would protect him, but he was ordered into irons, taken to Dublin, and brought before a court-martial where General Loftus sat as president. He appeared in full dress as a French officer. He had been taken in the act of bearing arms against his Sovereign. "In a cause like mine," he said, "success is everything. Success in the eyes of the vulgar is the test of merit. Washington succeeded; Kosciusko failed. I have forfeited my life. The court shall do its duty. I shall not be wanting in mine." Having been tried as a soldier, he begged he might have a soldier's death. The request was refused. He was sentenced to be hanged the following morning in front of the new prison. There was no time for an appeal, and in the night he cut his throat with a penknife. The execution was put off, and for another week Wolfe Tone lingered in pain and then died.

Another event still fresh in our memory is connected with Inishowen. During the great war many of the German submarines, submerged in its waters, lay in wait for British and American merchant vessels, and many a fine ship and gallant seaman lie buried in the deep sea around the coast.

About four miles from Derry is Culmore Fort. It was the great outpost of Derry and the principal fortress of Lough Foyle, but as a military station it has ceased to be used for the last 160 years. It was preserved from total dilapidation by Mr. Abraham M'Causland in 1785, and in 1824 General Hart repaired it in a permanent manner. The walls are more than six feet thick, and the tower consists of three storeys. The fortalice was built sometime in the sixteenth century, and is frequently mentioned in connection with the troubles in the North. In 1608, upon the breaking out of Sir Cahir O'Doherty's rebellion, it was surprised and treacherously taken by him.

A striking and authentic anecdote is recorded in Cox's "Hibernia Anghcana," which illustrates the daring and unscrupulous character of the young chieftain O'Doherty. After the death of Sir John O'Doherty, Cahir, his son, pretended great affection for the English, and particularly for the young officer who was the Governor of Culmore Fort, near Derry. Great trust was reposed in him, and he was soon made a Justice of the Peace and looked on as a sincere friend. Upon a certain day Sir Cahir invited the Governor to dinner. He came with his wife and little child, to whom Sir Cahir was godfather, to the chieftain's feast. After dinner O'Doherty arose and called the Governor aside and plainly told him that he hated the English, and that he must be revenged and have Culmore. "Surrender it quickly to me," he said to the Governor, "or yourself, your wife, and child must die." At this moment a band of armed kerns rushed into the room; the loyal Governor refused to yield up the fort, and Sir Cahir gave orders to his men to execute him.

At that instant, Lady O'Doherty and the wife of the Governor rushed into the room, and by their urgent entreaties dissuaded the chieftain from the murder. He, therefore, sent the Governor out of the room, well-guarded, and, addressing his wife, said: "Madam, go off instantly to Culmore with this band of soldiers; get them peaceably into the fort, or your husband and child must die." The distracted wife gave way. She went with the rebels to the castle and told the sentries that her husband had broken his leg. The sentry did not hesitate to admit her and her party, and when they had gained admission they murdered the garrison and took possession of the fort. The Governor's life was saved, but he was utterly ruined. Sir Cahir O'Doherty then marched on Derry, sacked and burnt it, and slew the Governor and garrison. This happened in 1608, but six months later he was finally worsted and his lands confiscated.

Not far from the village of Kilmacrennan is the Rock of Doon, the royal coronation place of the chieftains of Tyrconnell, and the scene of the death of Sir Cahir O'Doherty. It is a natural fortress in a very inaccessible district, and well suited for the retreat of these daring warriors.

Before the Plantation of Ulster several Scots settled between Mulroy Bay and Lough Foyle under the auspices of Rory O'Donnell, Earl of Tyrconnell. One Sandy Ramsay, obtained a grant in the valley of the Lennan, and built a bawn and residence. Sir Cahir O'Doherty and the Irish regarded these settlers with great hatred. During the absence of Ramsay upon one occasion, the chieftain made an attack upon his bawn, drove off the cattle, and slew his wife and children. Upon his return home the Scot found his newly-built bawn a smoking ruin, and his family slaughtered and himself bereft of all but his gun and dirk. Revenge became the passion of his soul. He knew there were 500 marks set upon the head of the rebel chieftain. Accordingly, he concealed himself from observation; he lurked about the haunts of the chief, and at last a fortunate opportunity presented itself.

On Holy Thursday, as the chief rested himself upon the eastern face of the Rock of Doon, little dreaming of danger, the Scot discovered him by his Spanish hat and heron plume, and, resting his gun upon a rock which concealed him from view, he applied the match, and the next moment the chieftain fell a lifeless corpse at the feet of a body of his retainers, who immediately fled, panic-stricken, which when the Scot observed he approached, and, severing the head from the body, wrapped it in his plaid and set off in the direction of Dublin.

But he was unfortunate in his speculation, for, sleeping in the cabin of one Terry Gallagher, near one of the fords of the Finn, the Irishman observed blood oozing through the pillow of his guest; he slit it open, and out rolled the reeking head. He instantly recognised the features, mounted his garron, and set off for Dublin, leaving the weary Scotsman dreaming of the reward he was never fated to receive.

O'Dohery rests beside the rock, where his grave is pointed out by the peasants, by whom his memory is still held in high respect.

Greencastle

THE old ruined castle at Grcencastle is perhaps one of the most interesting relics in Inishowen. It was also for centuries called Northburgh Castle. The castle was built in 1305 by Richard De Burgh (or Burke), the famous Red Earl of Ulster. Great estates in Ulster were granted to him by Edward II, and he built this castle to secure the entrance to Lough Foyle. Richard was defeated by Edward Bruce, brother of Robert, King of Scotland, at the battle of Connor, in Antrim, in 1315; but afterwards Bruce was defeated and slain at Faughart, near Dundalk, in 1318. Edward Bruce spent nearly a year in Greencastle. Richard De Burgh died in 1326, and was succeeded by his grandson, William, called the Dun (or Brown) Earl. He seized his relative, Walter De Burgh, confined him in Northburgh Castle, and starved him to death. Traces of the tragedy can be seen to this day. The affair made so deep an impression for centuries afterwards, that Walter's skeleton appears in the arms of the city of Derry as it was found in the castle dungeon after William's death. William was assassinated at the Fords of Belfast in 1333 by Sir Richard De Mandeville, brother-in-law of the starved Walter, in revenge. William left only one child, a daughter, who married Lionel, Duke of

Greencastle, Co. Donegal.

Clarence, son of Edward III. This ended the Norman power in the north-west of Ulster, where, however, it had never taken root. The castle then, thus deserted, fell into the hands of the chieftain of the great O'Doherty clan of Inishowen, and his successors held it for 250 years until the insane rebellion of Sir Cahir O'Doherty in 1608, already alluded to. After his death the clan lands in Inishowen were confiscated and granted by King James I to Sir Arthur Chichester, Lord Lieutenant of Ireland. His successors have held the lands, including the castle, ever since.

TORY ISLAND

TORY ISLAND lies about nine miles from the nearest point of Donegal. Its length is about three miles, and its breadth one. Its superficial contents are 1,200 acres, 200 of which are considered arable. The Commissioners of Irish Lights erected a lighthouse there in 1832, which is of great service to mariners, and has greatly diminished shipwrecks. It is visible in clear weather at a distance of 17 nautical miles, the lantern standing 122 feet above the level of the sea at high water. Before the erection of the lighthouse the inhabitants derived considerable profit from acting as pilots, and also from the timber thrown on shore.

The only place on the island where a few shrubs flourish is a hollow formed by the subsidence of the surface into a cavern beneath. Its Celtic designation is Lagrehy, or, "The Ram's Hollow." There are two villages on the island, East Town and West Town, the latter being the principal, and containing the round tower and the ecclesiastical ruins. The building materials are fragments of red granite, and the covering of the houses is thatch, kept down by ropes of straw and by stones. As limestone is not found on the island, the mortar, both ancient and modern, has been obtained by burning sea shells, chiefly those of the limpet, and the limpet is also used in large quantities as food and bait.

To a cursory observer, says an old writer who lived for a considerable time on the island some sixty years ago, and to whom I am indebted for information, the present dwellings have as much appearance of antiquity as the older buildings, and it is difficult to distinguish ancient from modern walls. In one place artificial caves are shown, said to have been formed during the war with France to conceal the people from the French, but more probably from English pressgangs, or, more likely still, they were used by smugglers before an excise steamer put an end to their traffic.

The most profitable business some seventy years ago was the manufacture of kelp from seaweed, and in 1845 the market was as much agitated on its small scale by the arrival of a few purchasers as some of the great marts where the wealth of nations is exchanged. The prosperity of this trade arises from the large proportion of iodine this kelp produces, which gives it a comparatively high value. Persons of every age and sex were employed collecting seaweed, or carrying it off the beach on the small island horses, in panniers having a movable bottom which drops down fin removing a pin; but I understand that this industry has in more modern days almost disappeared, and the population, which in the census of 1841 numbered nearly 400, has since that time considerably decreased.

There is neither resident magistrate, doctor, nor clergyman on the island, but a schoolmaster resides there under the auspices of the National Board. The people for the most part belong to the Roman Catholic Church. A clergyman from Cross Roads, on the opposite coast of Donegal, visits them periodically, or, in a case of urgency, a "curragh" is sent over to bring him. In his absence prayers are read on Sunday by one of the islanders at what is called St. John the Baptist's altar, near the round tower, and baptism is administered in cases of necessity.

It is said that when occasion requires more than usual deliberation on the part of the people, they elect a king. On one occasion when the august ceremony took place, it was for the purpose of considering whether geese should be allowed to be kept on the island, as complaints had been made that they injured the crops. A legislative decree was the result, banishing all geese for the future.

The "curragh" which is used by the islanders is one of the most primitive of boats, and from its buoyancy one of the safest when used by those accustomed to its management. The canoe formed from the hollow trunk of a tree may have preceded its use, but the raw hide of the newly-slain animal, properly extended, presented a readier means of constructing a boat, and became to the early inhabitants of the British Isles what the birch-tree bark is to the American Indians. Cæsar, Pliny, Claudian, Gildas, all refer to the "curragh." In these boats, according to Gildas, the Irish made their irruptions into Britain about A.D. 431 on the coast of the opposite mainland. The curraghs have generally sharp bows and square sterns, but those of a moderate size, intended to pass with safety through the long swell of the Atlantic, are square, or nearly so, at both extremities.

An old cutter's man stated that off the Shannon they often pull six oars, and that few boats can come up with them. He agreed in considering them the safest of all boats in the hands of men accustomed to their management. During all his experience in the Sound of Tory he never knew of one being lost, though they venture out in all waters. They are rowed with short oars or paddles, the smaller ones having two pairs-one man pulling a pair. They are what fishermen call club oars. Cattle are transferred across the Sound in these boats, and they are so light that a man easily carries one on his back.

Dr. Donovan, in a note on the battle of Moira, tells us that Tory Island is one of the earliest places mentioned in the Bardic History of Ireland, and is first referred to as the stronghold of the Formorians or African pirates who made many descents on the coast of Ireland at a period so far back in the night of time that it is now impossible to bring chronology to bear upon it. Tory was also one of the strongholds of the Scandinavians who ravaged the coasts of the British Isles and partially settled there. West Town in Tory Island is a quarry of remains of religious edifices.

It is generally understood that St. Columba introduced Christianity into this remote island and built a monastery there. The legend says, Columba, being admonished by an angel to cross into Tory, set sail with several other holy men for the island, that there arose a dissension among them with respect to the individual who should consecrate the island, and thereby acquire a right to it in the future, each renouncing from humility and a love of poverty the office of consecration and right of territory. They all agreed with St. Columba that the best way to settle it was by lot, and they determined by his direction to throw their staves in the direction of the island, with the understanding that he whose staff reached nearest to it should perform the office of consecration and acquire authority over Tory. Each threw his staff, but that of Columbkille, at the moment of issuing from his hand, assumed the form of a dart, and was borne to the island by supernatural agency.

The saint immediately called before him Alidus, son of the chief of the island, who refused to permit its consecration or the erection of any building. St. Columba then requested him to grant as much land as his outspread coat would cover. Alidus readily consented, conceiving the loss very trivial, but he had soon reason to change his mind, for the saint's cloak, when spread on the ground, dilated and stretched so much by its divine energy as to include within its border the entire island. Alidus was roused to frenzy by this circumstance, and incited or hunted upon the holy man a savage, ferocious dog, unchained for the purpose, which the saint immediately destroyed by making the sign of the Cross. The religious feelings of Alidus were awakened, by this miracle, says the legend. He threw himself at the saint's feet, asking pardon, and resigned to him the entire island.

No further opposition being made, St. Columba consecrated Tory, built a magnificent church, which he placed under the control of Eranus, one of his disciples. Among other things he commanded that no dog should ever again be introduced into the island. The ruins of the fine church he built are to be seen on the island to this day.

The O'Cahans of the Roe

In the English State Papers of 1515 there is a report about Ireland which is still extant. In that report it is said there were more than sixty separate States, some as big as a shire, some more, some less. In them there reigned more than sixty chief captains, "whereof some call themselves kings, some princes, dukes, and archdukes, that live only by the sword, and obey no other temporal person but only him that is strongest, and every one of the said captains makes war and peace for himself, and holds by the sword and obeys no other person, English or Irish, except only such persons as may subdue them by the sword." The country, it is said, was well governed under the native monarchs. Thus we are told of Brian Boru that under his rule equal justice was impartially administered; that he suffered no one to transgress the law. Warner, in his History of Ireland, describes the respect universally shown to the laws by the inhabitants by telling of a young damsel of surpassing beauty, robed in a costly dress, covered with jewels, carrying in her hand a wand, with a gold ring of great value fixed at the top, who wandered without attendants from the northernmost part of the island to the south, and that no one attempted, either in the face of day or under cover of night, to rob her of her honour or strip her of her rich apparel, or even steal her ring of gold.

On she went, and her maiden smile
In safety lighted her round the Green Isle;
And blessed for ever was she who relied
Upon Erin's honour and Erin's pride.

The Bawn at Dungiven.

Among the Irish chieftains of the North the O'Cahans of Dungiven and the Roe stand out conspicuously. Dermot O'Cahan, an Irish prince, was possessed of broad and extensive domains, hounded by the Bann, the Foyle, and the Northern Ocean. One of his castles, in which he frequently resided, was built on a rock overhanging the River Roe, on the site now known as the Dog's Leap, and nearly adjoining the Abbey of Drumachose. This prince had a lovely daughter named Finvola, and twelve sons, for whom he built twelve castles in different parts of his lands.

Archibald M'Spar ran tells how O'Cahan had frequent intercourse with the kings and princes of neighbouring nations, and with his daughter. Finvola visited the courts of Caledonia or Britain. I am indebted to his book for the narration which follows. On one occasion, returning from Caledonia with his son and Finvola, he was overtaken by a storm among the Western Isles, and nearly lost. They remained till the morning in distress, and then heard the rowing of a boat. In this boat appeared a young Highlander of bold and military carriage, who begged them to come with him. They came to a neighbouring castle at the farther verge of the island. "You are now," said the Highlander, "on the island of Islay." And also said O'Cahan, "the castle you are escorting us to is the castle of MacDonnell, Lord of the Isles." "The same," said the stranger. They were unwilling to go. "I pledge myself you will be welcome," said the stranger. They were met by the chief of the clan of MacDonnell, arrayed in full military costume, and got a hearty welcome. O'Cahan and the lovely Finvola were prevailed on to stay a few weeks.

The time arrived all too soon when the guests must return to Ireland, and young Angus MacDonnell sighed for Finvola. O'Cahan had ordered twelve castles to be built for his twelve sons, and wished to see how they were progressing. The monastery of Dooneven (Dungiven) was built by the ancestors of O'Cahan, and patronised by every succeeding proprietor. For the support of this monastery a voluntary allowance was given. Two men blindfolded started at the monastery, and as far as they could travel without falling was religiously set apart for the above purpose. One made two miles and then fell. The other made five miles, taking a westerly direction, until he reached a place called Com-Arg, where he also fell, this being the extremity of Dooneven parish. To the monastery of Dooneven were sent for education the youth of both sexes from the noblest families.

The first abbot who presided there was Paul O'Murray, a man deeply read in the learning of the times, and well acquainted with the Fathers. Under him were educated many of the Scottish MacDonnells, which was the principal cause of establishing a lasting friendship between them and the O'Cahans. The students here were daily instructed in the use of the broadsword and targe.

The universal pastime of those days was the pursuit of the hare, the stag, and the fox. It was the custom of the ladies also to join in the chase. Of all the favourite haunts of the stag in the country of O'Cahan, he chose the thickets overhanging the streams of the Roe, and, springing them, scaled the rugged heights of Ben Evenney. On one occasion the dogs found a wolf lying low. The dogs separated to right and left, and were bitten, but the wolf dashed on, and at last darted up the cliffs of Ben Evenney. The hunters thought it was the spirit of Ben Evenney, the guardian spirit of the OTahan family. "Who knows," said O'Cahan, at the feast on the hillside, "that the wolf which we hunted to-day from the neighbourhood of Dooneven has been only our great friend in disguise?"

MARRIAGE OF THE GEM OF THE ROE

Angus MacDonnell came unexpectedly, attended but by one servant, and was warmly received by
O'Cahan. He was coming on an embassy to ask the hand of Finvola, when he met Dermot O'Cahan and his men feasting at the foot of Ben Evenney. In a few days Angus delivered to the lady's father a letter from the Lord of the Isles making a proposal for his daughter, and asking as a dowry twenty-four chieftains' sons of the O'Cahans to be married to the daughters of as many chieftains of the MacDonnells. The contents of the letter were the subject of some days' meditation. The marriage was then solemnized in the abbey in presence of their friends and allies, who all came forward to greet the happy pair and bid a final farewell to Finvola, the gem of the Roe. The conditions on which Dermot O'Cahan parted with his daughter were that her remains when she died should be brought back and deposited in the old Abbey of Dooneven (Dungiven), the family burying-ground. These conditions being agreed upon, Finvola with her twelve maids and twenty-four gallant chevaliers set out for the Isles, leaving many a sorrowful heart behind them.

They lived happily together for many years, but at length Finvola passed away, and Angus, grieving deeply for her, did not wish it to be known to her people in the Roe. Yet Gramie Roe

O'Cahan, the banshee and guardian spirit of the family, howled it through the rugged caverns of Benbraddagh, beginning at twilight and plying the doleful lamentations through the night. Sir Angus MacDonnell could see the splendour of the torches which illumined the Firth as the vessel of the O'Cahan approached the shore. When they landed, a choir of females joined with Gramie Roe singing the death-song of Finvola, her beauty, her virtue, her high descent, asking why they did not bring her to the land of the O'Cahan, and not leave her among strangers.

The islanders, seeing the whole band surrounding the family burying-ground of MacDonnell, came swarming towards the mourners, and called aloud to prevent them raising the body. "Stand-off," said Turloughmore O'Cahan, who stood in the doorway of the cemetery with a ponderous sword in his hand, "stand-off, thou faithless islanders, who can pledge your vows to-day and break them to-morrow. The man wears not tartan in Morven dare force this pass, otherwise he shall bite the ground under my sword." "Who, proud Hibernian, art thou?" roared a tall Highlander from Glengarry, who bore a broadsword and targe. "Who art thou, I say?" and rushing forward threw a targe and cut deeply at him with a lusty arm. "No strife, my friends," said Sir Angus: "Finvola was honourably given to me. She came in love with me, and shall depart in the same. The fault was altogether mine, and if I have erred it was only through too much love."

The clan O'Cahan halted with Sir Angus during the following day, and then sailed for the Foyle with the remains of their much loved Finvola. At the close of the voyage her body was borne to Dungiven and reverently laid in the old Abbey of Dooneven, the resting-place of the O'Cahan family.

> *No more up the streamlet her maidens shall hie,*
> *For wan the cold cheek, and bedim'd the blue eye;*
> *In silent affliction our sorrows still flow,*
> *Since gone is Finvola, the gem of the Roe.*

COLERAINE

THE county now known as Londonderry was in early days known as the county of Coleraine. It was the territory of the O'Cahans, and extended from the Foyle to the Bann. The ancient possession of the O'Cahan family was granted by O'Neill, and was meted out to their chief in the following whimsical manner. O'Neill, in return for important services, granted to O'Cahan as far as his brown horse could run in a day, and also the fisheries of the Bann at Coleraine. Accordingly, starting from Burn Follagh, in the parish of Comber, he rode eastward to the Bann, which was henceforth to constitute his boundary in that direction. The power and authority of the family entitled them to the great distinction of holding the shoe over the head of O'Neill upon the day of his inauguration, the ceremony of which is thus recorded by Camden: "The O'Cahan was the greatest of the Uraights who held of the O'Neills, and being of the greatest authority in these parts he had the honour of holding the shoe over the head of the O'Neill, when chosen according to the rude ceremony then practised upon some high hill in the open air."

When Sir John Perrott, the Lord Deputy, formed seven counties of Ulster in 1586, the territory of Tyrone was broken up, and the northern part, called O'Cahan's country, became the county of Coleraine. The residence of the supreme chief was near Limavady, situated upon a high crag nearly 100 feet above the river, and adjacent to the cascade called Limavady, or the Dog's Leap, in the valley of the Roe. The castle is now erased from the face of the country, but its site, and the rath or fort by which it was defended on the land side, may still be traced.

The last of the O'Cahans was implicated in the Tyrone rebellion, and his estates forfeited. He was thrown into prison, and afterwards banished and his castle demolished. It was the wife of this O'Cahan that was visited by the Duchess of Buckingham, wife to the Earl of Antrim, her second husband. She had raised a levy of 1,000 men on the Antrim estates in aid of Charles I, and by order of the Deputy, Lord Westmeath, marched them to Limavady. Curiosity induced her to visit the wife of O'Cahan. The old lady continued to live in the ruined home of the family; she had kindled a fire of branches to keep off the rigours of the season within the roofless walls; the windows were stuffed with straw; and Lady O'Cahan herself was found by her noble visitor sitting on the damp ground in the smoke, wrapped in blankets, an affecting illustration of the ruined fortunes of her ancient and noble house. Her only son was sent to college by order of the King, but no trace has been found of him nor of his subsequent history.

This county was settled in 1618-19). From a paper printed in 1608, and given in the appendix of Sampson's Survey, we take the following curious and interesting particulars: The undertakers of the several proportions should be of three sorts- 1, English or Scottish, who were to plant their portions with inland Scots; 2, servitors in the Kingdom of Ireland who may take mere Irish or English or inland Scottish tenants; 3, natives of Ireland, who are to be made freeholders. The portions were to be distributed by lot.

The town of Coleraine, which is now the second in the county of Derry, formerly ranked as a city. According to Harris's

"Hibernica," and Pynar's Survey in 1618, "The county of Coleraine, otherwise called O'Cahan's county, was divided into 547 ballyboes, each ballyboe consisting of 60 acres; in all 34,187 acres." The town is a place of ancient note; its original name, according to Dr. Reeves in his' "Antiquities of Down and Connor," was "Cuil-rathain" (the ferny corner). For this etymology there is "The Tripartite Life of St. Patrick," which tells us that St. Patrick, having arrived in the neighbourhood, was hospitably entertained, and a piece of ground on the northern side of the Bann offered him whereon to build a church, in a spot overgrown with ferns. Bishop Cabreus, later on, chose this spot for his abode, from which circumstance it was ever afterwards called "Cuil Rathen" (the ferny retirement).

Others derive the name from "Cuil Rath Ean" (the fort at the bend of the river), a much more likely derivation. It was the head of an ancient bishopric. St. Columba visited Conallus, Bishop of Culerathen, by whom, as well as by the people, he was received with profound respect. But whether it fell into decay by slow degrees, or was destroyed by the Danes, it was of little note until it was again raised to the rank of a city by Sir John Perrott, the Lord Deputy, who laid it out on somewhat the same plan as Londonderry, with a large square in the centre of the town, called the Diamond or public square. In the vicinity of the town there was a very fine old fort called Mount Sandall, situated on a lofty eminence overhanging the River Bann, nearly over the Salmon Leap. This is generally supposed to have been the site of the great castle built by De Courcy in the year 1197, as mentioned by the Four Masters, and which was granted in 1215 by King John, along with the Castle Coulrath (Coleraine), to Thomas de Galweya.

Coming down to later times, it was the flight of the Earls of Tyrone and Tyrconnell from Lough Swilly, on the 14th September, 1607, that opened up the way for the great transformation called the "Plantation of Ulster." The province, alas, at this time was a howling wilderness; it could not be

The Salmon Leap.

otherwise after so many years of war and desolation. At a meeting of the Privy Council held in London at the close of 1612, the charter was duly prepared, and delivered two years after the city of London had committed itself to the undertaking of the Plantation. Two commissioners, Alderman Smithes and Mr. Springham, were sent to Ulster to inquire into the state of the Plantation and correct abuses. Their report, received in London in November, 1613, was not complimentary to those charged with the work of building. Derry and Coleraine were the first places that received the attention of the city's agents. Their report of Coleraine is of interest for the light it throws on the infant settlement; "The chiefest street was unpaved, and almost impassable; several houses were not plastered, and lying open they naturally had not attracted tenants; a general storehouse allowed the rain to pour through so shamefully that the contents were spoiled, firkins of butter decayed, cheese rotted, grievous to behold; nails sent from Derry in open baskets, and therefore rusty. Other houses were tenantless because of the high rates charged. The church, though it had a good attendance of worshippers, showed signs of neglect, and was unplastered. Its interior was described as 'fowle' and unhandsome, and the supply of pews scanty." A contrast indeed to the stately church of today, erected through the zeal and untiring energy of the late Bishop O'flara, who spent the evening of his days within view of the noble edifice which owes its existence to his pious zeal.

Three years later, in October, 1616, a more cheerful report was given of the progress of Coleraine. It had then, says the report, "ramparts made of earth and sods, along which ran a ditch filled, or soon to be filled, with water. There were also palisades from both sides of the fortifications made into the river, and two drawbridges done by our direction." Town planning also occupied the attention of the visitors. They suggested another row of houses answerable to the one in High Street, and said, "we wish them to be built of stone, so as to be defensible against the weather. We caused the Mayor to assemble the whole town, when we gave offer to give as many as will build a single house of stone, with three or four rooms, £20, and a lease thereof for 80 years, for a rent of 6s. 8d. per annum. We find there are 116 houses slated, but inhabited by 116 families having made two or three houses into one. Some others that were built of brick begin to decay, and the walls of others are by weather much decayed. We have given orders that the dormers thereof be slated as at Derry, which is as durable as stone. This will make them strong, where before they were of loam and lime, and ready to fall down."

Then, and for long afterwards, the difficulty of entering the Bann from the sea with vessels was a hindrance to the progress of the town, so that Portrush was regarded as the port of Coleraine. The offer made by the Commissioners in 1616 is worth nothing. " The bar is very dangerous. We saw Portrush so rocky and open to the north seas that it is very dangerous; but we make an offer that if the town and country will join together to make a good harbour there, that would be a means to the city, to give £200 towards that charge when it would be finished."

In the time of James I the Lord Deputy, Chichester, obtained a grant of the fisheries of the Bann. After wards the Government purchased back the grant in favour of the London Society. The rent paid to the Society was £900 a year. The expenses of management used to vary from £1,000 to £1,500. As to the quantities taken, it is stated that in one year 250 tons of fish were salted, besides what were sold fresh; the least take of any known year was 45 tons. As to prices, in 1957 salmon sold at 1d. a Ib.; for many years after at 1.5d. a lb.; at the end of the century it rose to 3d.; later still, to 3.5d. The salmon of the Bann have but one season, and must go sometimes thirty or forty miles to find a convenient place for spawning.

It may be of interest to notice the price of other provisions at this time. According to the Commissioners' report, the prices ruling in Ulster in 1616 were as follows:- For a cow or bullock, fifteen shillings, or about one halfpenny per lb.; a sheep, sixteen pence or two shillings; a hog, two shillings; barley, eleven pence per bushel; oats, four pence a bushel. These figures enable us to understand the value of labour when expressed in terms of £ s. d. The wages paid to a plough-holder were six shillings and eight pence a quarter, with meat and drink; for a leader of a plough, five shillings; for a cow-boy for two heifers, one penny per half year. Maintenance was evidently the chief return for the labourer's services. A good servant-maid got ten shillings a year; and a labourer's pay per day, with meat, was two pence, A master carpenter or mason received sixpence a day, if he had also meat and drink; but if he provided for himself he was allowed twelve pence per day. The price of the largest pair of brogues was only nine pence. No labourers were allowed to wander from one barony to another without a warrant from a justice of the peace, and no servant was to be hired for a shorter period than half-a-year. Such are some of the facts in the early history of Coleraine, as depicted by Mr. Doyle in his "Antiquities of Ireland," by Mr. Sampson in his Survey, and by Mr. Kernohan in a recent pamphlet.

Coleraine has advanced by leaps and bounds since those days, and can now proudly take its stand as one of the leading towns of Ulster. The story of its infant days is not without interest to its residents of to-day.

ENNISKILLEN

THIS place, which takes its name from the island in Lough Erne in which it is situated, and was formerly called Inniskillen, was, previously to the time of James I, merely a stronghold of Maguire, chieftain of Fermanagh, who had a castle here, which was taken by the English forces under Sir Richard Bingham in 1594; but no sooner had that general retired, leaving in it a royal garrison, than it was besieged by the forces of O'Donnell and his confederates. A detachment sent to its assistance by the Lord Deputy was totally defeated, and the garrison, after holding out to the last extremity, being compelled to surrender, were inhumanly slaughtered by the assailants, who pleaded the like cruelty on the part of Bingham when he took the town as a justification of their revenge.

The town, though it holds a conspicuous place in Irish history, and is now the capital of the county, is of no great antiquity. The island, being considered an important spot for the establishment of a military force, a royal fort was erected there about the commencement of the seventeenth century, and the advantage of its situation for a town induced King James I in 1612 to make a grant of one-third of it to William Cole, Esq., ancestor of the Earl of Enniskillen, on condition of his building a town upon it, settling in it twenty British families to be incorporated as burgesses-some of whose descendants still hold burgage tenements-and assigning convenient places for a church and churchyard, a market house, public school, thirty acres for a common, and a site for a prison to be built for the custody of prisoners and malefactors within the limits of the county of Fermanagh. This last condition seems to imply that it was intended to make this the assize town and capital of the county from the very date of its foundation.

Enniskillen.

During the war of the Revolution the inhabitants firmly adhered to the cause of William III, whom they proclaimed King. Enniskillen, though the capital of the county of Fermanagh, was then merely a village. It consisted of about eighty dwellings, clustering round an ancient castle. The inhabitants were, with scarcely an exception, of the Protestant faith. Early in December they received an intimation from Dublin that two companies of King James's infantry were to be immediately quartered on them. A daring resolution was taken-come what might, the troops should not be admitted. Yet the means of defence were slender. Not ten pounds of powder, not twenty fire-locks fit for use, could be collected within the walls. Messengers were sent with pressing letters to summon the gentry of the neighbourhood to the rescue, and the summons was gallantly obeyed. In a few hours 200 foot and 150 horse assembled. Gustavus Hamilton, a gentleman who had served in the army, but who had recently been deprived of his commission by Tyrconnell, was appointed Governor, and took up his residence in the castle. Trusty men were enlisted and armed with great expedition. As there was a scarcity of swords and pikes, smiths were employed to make weapons by fastening scythes on poles. All the country houses round Lough Erne were turned into garrisons.

It was determined at Dublin that an attack should be made on Enniskillen from several quarters at once. Macarthy marched towards Lough Erne from the east with three regiments of dragoons and some troops of cavalry. A considerable force was at the same time to advance from the west. The Duke of Berwick was to come from the north with such horse and dragoons as could be spared from the army which was besieging Londonderry.

The Enniskilleners had sent a petition to Captain Kirke, who was in command of the ships in Lough Foyle, to ask for help. Kirke could not spare soldiers, but he sent some arms, ammunition, and several experienced officers, of whom the chiefs were Colonel Wolseley and Lieutenant-Colonel Berry. These officers came by sea round the coast of Donegal, and ran up the Erne. On Sunday, 29th July, 1689, it was known that their boat was approaching the island of Enniskillen, The whole population came to the shore to greet them. It was with difficulty that they made their way to the castle through the crowds which hung on them, blessing God that dear old England had not quite forgotten the men who upheld her cause against odds in the heart of Ireland.

Wolseley had scarcely taken on himself the chief command when he received notice that Lord Mountcashel had laid siege to the castle of Crum, which was the frontier garrison of the Protestants of Fermanagh. The ruins of the old fortress are now among the attractions of a beautiful pleasure-ground, situated on a woody promontory which overlooks Lough Erne. He sent

Berry forward with such troops as could be instantly put in motion, and promised to follow speedily with a large force.

Berry, after marching some miles, encountered thirteen companies of Macarthy's dragoons, commanded by Anthony, the most brilliant and accomplished of all who bore the name of Hamilton, but much less successful as a soldier than as a courtier, a lover, and a writer. Hamilton's dragoons ran at the first fire, and he himself was severely wounded. His second in command was shot dead. Macarthy soon came up to support Hamilton, followed by Wolseley to support Berry. The hostile armies were now in presence of each other. Macarthy had over five thousand men and several pieces of artillery. The Enniskilleners were under three thousand, and they had marched in such haste that they had brought only one day's provisions. It was, therefore, absolutely necessary for them either to fight instantly or to retreat. Colonel Wolseley determined to consult the men. The ranks were drawn up under arms, and the question was put, "Advance or retreat?" The answer was a universal shout of "Advance!"

Colonel Wolseley instantly made his dispositions tor an attack. As he approached, the enemy, to his great surprise, began to retire. The Enniskilleners were eager to pursue with all speed; but their commander, suspecting a snare, restrained their ardour, and positively forbade them to break their ranks. Thus one army retreated and the other followed in good order through the little town of Newtownbutler. About a mile from that town the soldiers of King James faced about and made a stand. Their position was well chosen. They were drawn up on a hill, at the foot of which lay a deep bog. A narrow, paved causeway which ran across the bog was the only road by which the cavalry of the Enniskilleners could advance, for on the right and left were pools, turf pits, and quagmires, which afforded no footing to horses. Macarthy placed his cannon in such a manner as to sweep this causeway. Colonel Wolseley ordered his infantry to the attack. They struggled through the bog, made their way to firm ground and rushed on the guns. There was then a short and desperate fight. The Irish cannoners stood gallantly to their pieces till they were cut down to a man. The Enniskillen horse, no longer in danger of being mowed down by the fire of the artillery, came fast up the causeway. The Irish dragoons were smitten with another panic, and, without striking a blow, galloped from the field.

Such was the terror of the fugitives that many of them spurred hard till their beasts fell down, and then continued to fly on foot, throwing away carbines, swords, and even coats, as encumbrances. The infantry, seeing themselves deserted, flung down their pikes and muskets, and ran for their lives. Nearly 1,500 were put to the sword. About 500 more, in ignorance of the country, took a road which led to Lough Erne. The lake was before them, the enemy behind; they plunged into the waters and perished there. Macarthy, abandoned by his troops, rushed into the midst of the pursuers, and very nearly found the death which he sought. He was wounded in several places; he was struck to the ground, and in another moment his brains would have been knocked out with the buttend of a musket, when he was recognised and saved. The Enniskilleners lost only 20 men killed and 50 wounded. They took 400 prisoners, 7 pieces of cannon, 14 barrels of powder, all the drums and all the colours of the vanquished enemy. The battle of Newtownbutler was won on the same afternoon on which the boom thrown over the Foyle was broken.

Such was the defence of the men of Enniskillen in July, 1689, which stands side by side with that of Derry in grateful remembrance by their countrymen.

DUNGANNON

DUNGANNON, once the capital of County Tyrone, is a place of great antiquity. It appears to have been the chief seat of the O'Nials or O'Neills from the earliest period of Irish history. The first direct notice of it under its present name is in the spirited letter addressed in 1329 to Pope John from Dungannon by Donald O'Neill, in which he styles himself "King of Ulster and true heir of the whole dominion of Ireland." He declares that previously to the coming of St. Patrick one hundred and thirty of his royal ancestors had been Kings of Ireland, and from that period till the landing of King Henry II in 1172 "sixty monarchs of the same princely family had swayed the Hibernian sceptre." In 1364 O'Nial, in his letters to King Edward III, styles himself "Prince of the Irishry in Ulster." In 1538 Con O'Nial took up arms against Henry VIII in favour of the See of Rome, marched from Dungannon with a powerful army into the English pale, and laid waste the country as far as Meath, where lie was met by Lord Deputy Grey, who defeated him at Bellahoe, and compelled him again to retreat to his stronghold of Dungannon. Soon after this he submitted to the English authority and in 1542 took the oaths of allegiance.

After this battle Henry VIII assumed the title of King instead of Lord of Ireland; and Con O'Nial covenanted to renounce the name of O'Nial, to adopt the English habit and language, and to build houses and farm the lands after the English mode. For this submission he was created Earl of Tyrone. His natural son, Matthew, was made Baron of Dungannon. Shane O'Neill, the lawful son, and his brothers were jealous of Matthew, and conspired against him. At the beginning of April, 1562, the young Baron of Dungannon was waylaid in a wood near Carlingford by Tirlogh O'Neill. He fled for his life, with the murderers behind him, till he reached the banks of a deep river, which he could not swim, and there he was killed. Soon after this Shane O'Neill conspired against his father, deposed him, and drove him into the Pale, where he afterwards died. Shane then threw over his English title, and, professing to prefer the name of O'Neill to any patent of nobility held under an English Sovereign, he claimed the right of succession by Irish custom, precedent, and law. Shane was now successful everywhere. The Maguire had to flee from his islands, the castle of the O'Donnells was surrendered, the English garrison at Armagh was withdrawn, and at last, over river, bog, and mountain, Shane was undisputed Lord of Ulster.

O'Neill's Old Castle, Dungannon.

"The only strong man in Ireland," he administered justice after a paternal fashion, permitting no robbers but himself. When wrong was done he compelled restitution. Two hundred pipes of wine were stored in his cellars, six hundred men-at-arms fed at his table- "as it were his janissaries" and daily he feasted the beggars at his gate.

Shane had now reached the summit of his power, but dark days were in store for him. A joint movement was concerted between the new Deputy, Sir Henry Sidney, and the O'Donnells; and while the Deputy, with the light horse of the Pale, overran Tyrone and carried off three thousand cattle, Hugh O'Donnell came down on Shane on the river that runs into Lough Foyle. It was somewhere, perhaps, between Lifford and Londonderry, on the west side of the river. After a brief sight the O'Neills broke and fled; the enemy was behind them, the river was in front, and when the Irish battle-cries had died away over moor and mountain, only two hundred survived of those fierce troopers who were to have cleared Ireland for ever from the presence of the Saxons. For the rest, says Froude, the wolves were snarling over their bodies, and the seagulls wheeling over them with screams and cries as they floated down to their last resting-place beneath the quiet waters of Lough Foyle. Shane's foster brethren, faithful to the last, were all killed. He himself, with a few comrades, rode for his life, pursued by the avenging furies.

In the far extremity of Antrim, sheltered among the hills and close upon the sea, lay the camp of Alister MacDonnell and his nephew, Gillespie. Here, on Saturday the last day of May, appeared Shane O'Neill and some fifty men, and threw themselves on the hospitality of Alister. They were received with kindness; but on the third evening, soon after supper, when the wine and whiskey had gone freely round, and the blood in Shane's veins had warmed again, a quarrel arose, fierce words were spoken; Gillespie sprang to his feet, ran out of the tent, and raised the slogan of the isles. A hundred dirks flashed in the moonlight, and the Irish, wherever they could be found, were struck down and stabbed. Some two or three found their horses and escaped; all the rest were murdered, and Shane himself, gashed with fifty wounds, was wrapped in a kern's old shirt and flung into a pit hastily dug among the ruined arches of Glenarm. Even there, what was left of him was not allowed to rest. Four days later the captain of Knockfergus hacked the head from the body, and carried it on a spear's point through Drogheda to Dublin, where, staked upon a spike, it bleached on the battlements of the Castle. So died Shane O'Neill, a keen and fiery patriot, the representative in his birth of the line of the ancient Kings; the ideal in his character of all which Irishmen most admire; regardless in his actions of the laws of God and man, yet the devoted subject in his creed of the Roman Catholic Church, with an eye which could see far beyond the limits of his own island, and a tongue which could touch the most passionate chords of the Irish heart.

Hugh O'Neill, son of the Baron of Dungannon, escaped when his father was murdered. He was educated in England, and became a favourite of Queen Elizabeth. He was raised to the earldom of Tyrone, and built a fine castle at Dungannon; but later on, meditating new designs against England, he was discovered, and, dreading the power of King James I, he fled to the continent in 1607, leaving the whole of his extensive possessions to the King, who in 1610 granted the castle and manor of Dungannon, with all their dependencies, to Sir Arthur Chichester.

In 1612 Sir Arthur obtained from the King a charter of incorporation for the town which he was about to build, a grant of 1,140 acres of land, and of 500 acres more for the site of the intended town. Upon the former he built a bawn of limestone 120 feet square, with bulwarks and a deep fosse; and upon the latter, previously to 1619, six large stone houses, six strong houses of framework timber, and a spacious church, with the exception of the roof, was completed at that time, whence may be dated the origin of the present town.

On the breaking out of the war in 1641, Sir Phelim O'Neill, having taken the fort of Charlemont by stratagem, and made the governor prisoner, seized the castle, town, and fort of Dungannon on the same night, and, having put many of the inhabitants to death, kept possession of it till after the battle of Benburb in 1646, when the town and church were burnt; subsequently the castle was dismantled by order of the Parliament. It was rebuilt after the Restoration, and was garrisoned in 1646 by the troops of James II, who, on the 13th of April in that year, visited the town and inspected the garrison, whence he marched to Omagh and Strahane, but his forces occupied the town and neighbourhood during the whole of that important struggle. From this period the only event of historical importance connected with the town is the meeting of the delegates from 269 corps of Ulster Volunteers, who in 1782 assembled at Dungannon, and passed twenty resolutions declaratory of the independence of the Parliament of Ireland. Dungannon is situated about three miles from the south shore of Lough Neagh, and is a spacious, handsome, and well-built town. It consists of a square and four principal and several smaller streets. The situation of the town, on a lofty hill of limestone, renders it both a healthy and pleasant place of residence. The Royal School was founded by letters patent of James I. It is situated on a gentle eminence on the east side of the town, on grounds comprising nine acres, purchased by Primate Robinson and given to the school.

Part Two
On the Sea Coast of Derry, Antrim and Down

DOWNHILL AND CASTLEROCK

DOWNHILL stands on a cliff 250 feet above the sea. Looking northward the waters of the Atlantic stretch to the horizon. To the west is Inishowen Head, which receives, at the entrance to Lough Foyle, the full shock of the waves to the north; while, in the direction of Scotland, the Isles of Mull, Islay, and Jura are visible in the distance. Downhill, built by the Earl of Bristol, Bishop of Deny, is the house which Charles Lever describes in his novel "The Bramleighs of Bishop's Folly," though the story has no historic connection with the house or its inmates. But Lever knew this "Bishop's Folly " in the days when he was a dispensary doctor at Portstewart.

Yet one who has known and loved it from childhood writes of it in a different strain: "There can be but one Downhill. It is unique both in situation and design. "So exposed is the situation of the house, that no trees will grow in its neighbourhood. In contrast to the bleak exposure of the house is the adjacent "glen" which encloses a lawn in the form of a horse-shoe, where trees and ferns grow in profusion, and a little river runs clear and still, so protected is this oasis from the winds which rage outside it. The material used for the building of Downhill was in great measure drawn from the quarries of the county; while the work during many years gave employment to vast numbers of labourers.

The Bishop's taste in architecture, as exemplified by Downhill and Ballyscullion, was strongly influenced by classical and Italian models. He erected a mausoleum in the grounds, at a cost of £5,000, to the memory of his brother, George, Earl of Bristol, whose death occurred in 1775, and to whose title the Bishop eventually succeeded. The mausoleum, the remains of which still exist, standing in its own grounds between the Bishop's Gate and the Lion's Gate, was originally surmounted by a dome, supported by eight columns, beneath which stood Van Vost's fine statue of the earl. The whole of the top of this fine work of art was unfortunately destroyed by a gale in 1839. A portion of Downhill, with the greater part of the collections it contained, was destroyed by fire in the middle of the nineteenth century.

Of the Bishop's friends, Mr. James Bruce, who was married to his cousin, was a special favourite. On the death of their parents the Bishop took charge of the children. The two sons were younger than the sister. The elder, Henry Hervey Bruce, in after years became rector of Tamlaghtfinlagan parish, and eventually succeeded to the whole of the Bishop's Irish property. Miss Bruce, to whom the Bishop was specially devoted, married in 1781 Daniel Mussenden, Esq., of Larchfield, Co. Down. She died two years after, at the age of 22. Downhill still evokes her memory by traces of her brief association with the place.

A romantic interest attaches to the Mussenden Temple, as it is called to-day. Domed and circular, it resembles Bramante's Temple of Monte Granicolo at Rome, and stands on the edge of a cliff overlooking the Atlantic ocean. Though wind and storm and fire have wrought havoc on other monuments of the Bishop at Downhill, this will remain a memorial of a lovely woman cut off in early prime, and of the Bishop's romantic tribute to her perfections. Planting and farming at Downhill were a source of interest to the Bishop, and he was also interested in the welfare of the 300 labourers in his employment. "Downhill," he mentions in one of his letters, "is in greater beauty than ever, and 300,000 trees have been planted without one of them failing." The years which he passed here were the palmy days of his prosperity. Later, after the death of Mrs. Mussenden, his residence there was fitful and unsettled.

The Bishop has been looked upon as more or less eccentric, and a man of many moods; but he had decidedly a humorous side to his character. A Presbyterian minister, the Rev. Classon Porter, has recorded a tradition that, on one beautiful summer evening, the Bishop proposed after dinner to his numerous guests, that they should adjourn from the dinner table to the splendid strand of Magilligan, which is immediately below Downhill. The idea was cordially adopted, and the entire party went out to stroll on the beach. As they passed the stables the Bishop, unobserved, ordered his grooms to saddle all the horses, of which he had a great number, and bring them down to the strand. He then proposed that his clergy and the Presbyterian ministers should forthwith ride together, two and two, a series of equestrian races on the beach, and that he himself should start the several batches of competitors. Thus challenged, his guests could not well refuse, and the rival clergy had nothing for it but to run the races. In every instance the Presbyterian ministers were victorious. The clergy of the Established Church were generally large, portly men, more accustomed to drive than to ride, and many of them tumbled off their horses.

If the Bishop had no great regard for the wealthier members of his clergy, some of whom resided far away from their parishes, he was extremely considerate to poor curates. He set apart for their special accommodation a large suite of rooms at Downhill, which he called "The Curates' Corridor"- it is so called to this day-and they were always the most welcome guests at his table. Mr. Saurin, a curate, had a toast he was in the habit of giving at Downhill. It was a toast which embodied a wish, perhaps not unnatural for a curate to entertain, but one that few curates would have had the candour to avow. It was simply, "A rot among the Rectors." The idea always amused the Bishop, and in due course he made Mr. Saurin a rector. When that gentleman was dining at Downhill for the first time after he got his rectory, the Bishop as usual called on him for his toast, saying: "I believe, Mr. Saurin, there is a toast which you have been in the habit of giving us on these occasions; if you please, we will have it now." "Oh, my Lord," said the newly-appointed rector, "since I had the pleasure of dining here your Lordship has given me reason to change my toast. I ask you no longer to drink 'A rot among the Rectors'; I ask you to drink 'Patience among the Curates'!"

Whatever may be thought of the Bishop's political career, it seems not too much to claim for him that he was both disinterested and consistent in his political aims. "He was certainly sincere," says Sir Jonah Barrington, himself an honest patriot. There was one underlying tone which pervaded every serious thought and action in his life; if in nothing else, he was earnest and consistent in this through life-he strove unceasingly for toleration and freedom in religion and politics, and against tyranny and oppression wherever it was found. He rebuilt the Bishop's Palace in Derry, and laid out a bishop's garden on the old ground of St. Columb's monastery; he also helped to build many a church and raise many a spire; and he never spared his pocket in laying down a new road or in building a glebe house, or in any work of charity or philanthropy.

CASTLEROCK.

Nestling at the foot of the hill on which Downhill Castle stands, lies the little village of Castlerock. It forms part of the Bruce estate. It is trim and clean, and sufficiently primitive to be an ideal spot for a tired city dweller to spend a happy holiday. Good houses and rooms are to be had for the summer months, and comfortable, homely hotels. A long stretch of sand extends to the mouth of the river Bann, where children can have a happy time. There is an excellent, well-kept golf course of 18 holes, over which championship matches have been frequently played; also a charming little club-house, where refreshments may be had. There are also tennis courts, and every facility for bathing, both in deep and shallow water. For those who want pure sea air and beautiful scenery, it would be difficult find a prettier spot than Castlerock. The fisherman, too, will find plenty of salmon trout, and boats, if required, at the mouth of the River Bann, about half a mile from the village.

PORTSTEWART

THE town of Portstewart lies on the slope of a hill, semi-circular in shape and dipping down to the sea. There are no extremes in climate. The east wind in the spring-, with its biting cold, is shut out, and in the summer the heat is tempered by the cool breezes from the Atlantic. Although Portstewart was widely known as a watering-place when Portrush was a mere fishing village, its foundation dates back only to the middle of the eighteenth century. The land originally belonged to the Stewarts of Ballylease-a branch of the Royal Stewarts, who came from Scotland and settled at Ballintoy. John Cromie, of Cromore, married Miss Stewart of Ballylease, and, on the death of the last male representative of the family, the estate passed into his hands. Mr. Cromie built the first slated house at Portstewart in 1790. During the next thirty years the village consisted of a few fishermen's huts. Mr. John Cromie, son of the first named, commenced to erect good houses for the accommodation of summer visitors, and in conjunction with the O'Hara family, owners of the adjoining property, great improvements were carried out, and many of the gentry of County Derry provided themselves with houses for summer use. The original parish church, situated about a mile from the town, owed its existence to the O'Neill family-a branch of the O'Neills of Shane's Castle-which flourished in the neighbourhood for generations. About a hundred years ago a new church was built on the triangular plot which now serves as the new graveyard; but the people of Portstewart, which was then growing into importance, considered that a more convenient site should have been chosen. They refused to walk to Agherton, and the ecclesiastical authorities had the building pulled down and re-erected in its present position in 1826.

Portstewart in1822.

The first harbour was constructed in 1832 at an outlay of £1,200. It admitted vessels of 50 tons, and served its purpose up to 1889, when enlargements and improvements were carried out by the Board of Works. The present fine dock was added in 1910. Portstewart has an intimate connection with Dr. Adam Clarke, the eminent oriental scholar and Biblical commentator.

In 1832, when the town was without a rival as a watering-place in Ulster, Charles Lever, author of the Lorrequer novels, which contain fine descriptions of military life, came from Dublin to take charge of the cholera hospital at Coleraine. He remained there but a few months, and then went as dispensary doctor to Portstewart. He and his wife lived at Verandah Cottage, the site of which is now occupied by Lever House. In his "Knight of Gwynne" there are many allusions to Portstewart and its people, of whom Lever entertained the kindliest recollections. A few years before his death, when he had experienced to the full of the joys and sorrows of life, he told a friend that he regretted that he had ever ceased to be the humble dispensary doctor of Portstewart. As an oral storyteller, Lever is described as excelling in charm anything ever produced by his pen. At every party his presence was joyfully hailed. The guests never separated until he had organised two or three picnic excursions to the Skerries, to Dunluce Castle, to Dunmull Hill and its Druidical circle, to Beardiville and its pagan altar, the Giant's Causeway, or the rope bridge at Carrick-a-rede. "Perhaps in all the seaboard of the Empire," he wrote, "nothing of the same extent can vie in awful sublimity with this iron-bound coast." For many years after he left to take up a position as physician to the British Legation at Brussels, the country was full of stories of "the wild young doctor" who himself performed in Coleraine the feat of jumping over a horse and cart, which Lever attributed to Charles O'Malley at Lisbon. He is also described as riding to and fro the entire night between the bed of a child dangerously ill and a ball given by the officers of a regiment then at Coleraine, and that, too, in evening dress. Thackeray, during his Irish visit in 1842, visited Portstewart, and gives an account of his visit in his "Irish Sketch Book,"

It appeared to him that the whole place had an air of comfort and neatness which was seldom seen in Ireland.

It was intended that the Ballymena and Portrush Railway, which opened in 1858, should go through Portstewart, but, owing to the opposition of Mr. Cromie, who feared that the method of travelling would lead to Sunday desecration, the line was diverted to within a mile and a half of the town. The townspeople deeply regret Mr. Cromie's obstinacy on this point, and he himself was wont to admit that he had made a mistake in opposing the original intention of the promoters.

Little now remains of old Portstewart but the two thatched cottages at the base of the castle wall- the last of the Bone Row, so called because the inhabitants fastened the thatch with the bones of fish instead of wooden pegs-and a few thatched houses on the Coleraine Road. Its bathing facilities, water supply, electric light, and its two interesting golf courses would reflect credit on many a richer and larger community - all uniting not only to make Portstewart one of the most desirable watering-places, but also an ideal spot for permanent residence. Mr. Cromie became the ground landlord of the whole of Portstewart by purchase. His daughter married Lord Robert Montagu, son of the Duke of Manchester, through whom the estates descended to the present owner - Mr. R. A. C. Montagu.

PORTRUSH

PORTRUSH is supposed to have derived its name from Portruis (the port of the promontory). It was named " Portrosse " in the twelfth century, and before that it was called Cuan-ard-Corran (point of the high corner). About 150 years ago there were only a few houses there, most of them at the harbour end of the town, above the port. The inhabitants were chiefly fishermen and pilots. Archdeacon Pococke passed through Portrush in 1752, and it may be that the inhospitable character of the port at that time accounts for the unfavourable impression left on his mind after a visit to the now bright and popular watering-place. "Portrush," he says, "is a little creek encompassed with sandy banks which gain in the land as the sands do in Cornwall. Though it is well sheltered, yet there runs such a sea that it is not safe for the boats in winter. This little town is of so little consequence that there is not a public house in it for accommodation of travellers. They have but one merchant in the town, who deals chiefly in shipping of corn and kelp." About the same time, 1750 to 1760, emigrant ships lay in the shelter of the Skerries.

Portrush was greatly frequented by French fishermen from Brest and St. Malo in the seventeenth and eighteenth centuries, who always came there in the spring to fish cod, ling, ray, and dogfish, which they cured and took to the markets of France and Spain. There was a young woman named Mary Murphy who lived in Portrush in the reign of William III. It is said she stood seven feet two inches without shoes or headgear. She married the captain of one of these French fishing vessels, who took her to France and afterwards to London, where she was exhibited in Fleet Street as a giantess. Queen Mary heard of her and invited her to visit Kensington Palace, where it is said she danced an Irish jig, and sang an Irish song to the King and Queen, who were greatly pleased with her. An English gentleman saw her in Portrush in 1696, she being then 23 years of age; and again, in 1701, he saw her in France exhibited at a fair. When Miss Murphy was dressed for the show she was exceedingly handsome, and looked much taller than she really was, as she was admirably proportioned. It is said that a hermit named MacGilladhu (or Black), who lived in Portcoon Cave at the Giant's Causeway, fell in love with this fair girl, who declined to return it; and upon hearing that a foreigner had carried her off he fell sick and died, and was buried at Mount Sandal, near Coleraine, to which it is said he belonged.

Portrush was one of the places which, in still earlier days, was coveted by Sir Thomas Phillips, who lived in the time of James I. The following is a summary of a letter he wrote to Sir Robert Cecil, the English Chief Secretary, dated May 19th, 1605: "Sir Randal McDonnell, upon our first acquaintance, being in good humour, gave me a little neck of land called Portrush, some mile and a half from the castle of Den Lewes [Dunluce]; it contains some sixty acres or thereabouts. When he gave them he conditioned I should keep the 'Red-shanks' from landing there, which I undertook, and have at my own charge made it defensive against them or any others his Majesty's enemies."

Later, on 22nd September, 1607, Phillips again writes to Lord Salisbury:- He is of opinion that his Majesty should fortify

Knockfergus, Port-Rush, and Lough Foyle, and then draw all the cows and other provisions out of the woods into the plains near these strong garrisons, where they may be fetched in upon the first news of any forces landing. This will be not only a means to starve them, but will save his Majesty a great sum in provisions for his army. He gives a scheme for fortifying Port-Rush and making it almost an island, so that 6,000 men might be embattled there. The Earl of Tyrone, to his knowledge, held it to be a place of importance.

The town lies within the shelter of Ramore Hill, a noble headland forming a peninsula consisting of a very marked and picturesque rock, which has long been a subject of interest to geologists, and for a considerable time the occasion of a warm geological controversy - Dr. Richardson maintaining that it was composed of basalts, containing pectinites, belemnites, and cornua ammonis. These show that they were formed in the bottom of the sea; and, relying upon this, he concludes that the basalts were once fluid and of aqueous origin. Professor Playfair, who visited the rock in company with Lord Webb Seymour and Sir James Hall, considers that he discovered the true solution of the difficulty, and ascertained that the part of the rock containing fossils was not basalt at all, but a stratum of slate clay and schist, forming a schistose of a high degree of induration by the vicinity of the ignited mass of whinstone. This has been confirmed by Conybeare and Buskland, 1813, and especially by Mr. Bryce, of Belfast, in his able paper upon the "Celebrated Portrush Rock," published in the first volume of the journal of the Geological Society of Dublin.

This hill in the last quarter of the nineteenth century was the fashionable promenade for visitors to Portrush, and the magnificent view of land and sea extending over 90 miles is very fine. Alongside Ramore Hill there was, in early days, another hill, which has since disappeared, known as Crannagh Hill. It was about twenty feet higher than the highest part of Ramore. It stood where the coal yards now are, on the north side of the

Portrush in 1822.

harbour, and was all quarried away to help to make the pier. There were steps up to the hill on the north side, and large cavities scooped out of the side of it in three places, wherein were seats, and no matter how the wind blew there was shelter at Crannagh Hill. This was the principal watch-house of the old pilots of Portrush. Mr. W. Adams tells us that before the new harbour was made there was a large fleet of smacks carrying salmon from Ballina and Ballyshannon to Liverpool. This was before steamboats began to run, and these vessels called at Portrush to re-ice. Often when they reached Portrush in their voyages the ice had melted, and they had to come and get moored in shelter off " Paddy's Pier," which was outside of what is now called the Old Dock-the only harbour at that time. There was always a squad of the strongest men about the "Port" picked to re-ice. The work had to be done in a great hurry, and the men were well paid for the job. The smacks were never long detained, and often went to sea in tempestuous weather. There was a prize of £5 for the first vessel to reach Liverpool. The prize was generally won by a smack called the "Benbulbin Hawk" which was manned by a Portrush crew; each smack carried five hands.

The new harbour was completed early in 1827, at a cost of £16,225 17s. 11d., raised under an Act of Parliament in shares of £100 each. A steamboat called the "St. Columb" was put on to run to Glasgow; and another, called the "Finn MacCool," shortly after, to run to Liverpool, about the year 1845. At tins time there were no railways between Coleraine, Belfast, and Derry, and nearly all Coleraine and Ballymoney goods came from Portrush.

In former days a castle stood on an eminence above the harbour, north of Crannagh Hill, looking seawards. It was called Castle-an-Teenie (or Castle of the Fire), from the fact that a bright light shone from it on dark stormy nights, which, tradition says, was withdrawn when anyone approached-possibly when any unknown vessel neared the rocks below. Bishop Reeves, in his "Antiquities" mentions that the castle was built by an ancient family named O'Corr, and that in A.D. 676 an O'Corr of Portrush joined hands with the son of the King of Dalriada in a battle with foreigners-probably the Norwegians-near Cuan-ard-Corran (Portrush).

An ancient abbey formed stood on the site of the Northern Counties Hotel and its lawn. In alluding to it, Bishop Reeves writes that the church of Portrush was valued in 1262, in the time of Pope Nicholas, at a yearly tax of £25. The walls were still standing at the beginning of the nineteenth century, and used as a shelter for fishermen. So late as 1884 portions of the walls were unearthed, with quantities of human bones.

About a mile and a quarter from Portrush stand the ruins of Ballywillin old church. This is one of the remaining old churches of the fourteenth century in Ireland. There is a large lancet window in the western gable, and other similar windows, most of which are built up. There are interesting monumental remains in the churchyard. One of the graves is said to be that of a daughter of James II. In 1641 the Rev. Donough O'Murray took refuge with his flock in this church and locked the great oaken door; but General Munro brought a small cannon against the door and forced them out, and Donough O'Murray agreed to sign the oath of allegiance to the English Government.

Ballywillin takes its name from Baile- Whillin (the town of the mill). The church was restored towards the end of the eighteenth century, and was used as a place of worship by the members of the Anglican Church till 1842, when Holy Trinity Church was built in Portrush.

The Clarke obelisk was erected in 1859 by admirers of Dr. Adam Clarke, a popular Wesley an minister and a famous expositor of the Bible. Some years earlier, in 1831, a piece of ground was given by the Earl of Antrim to build a little Methodist church. It was used for a school on weekdays and for a church on Sundays, and from the belfry of this little church most likely proceeded the first sound of the churchgoing bell heard for generations in Portrush, as there had been no place of worship in the village itself since 1642. The same bell, which is still heard every Sunday, was presented to the Duke of Newcastle by the Emperor Alexander of Russia. The Duke of Newcastle made a present of it to Dr. Adam Clarke, who gave it for the use of the Wesley an church.

Portrush

Another interesting ruin is Dunferte Castle, known by the name of the Castle of Ballyreagh, the townland in which it is situated. There now remains only a portion of the south wall, three feet in thickness and perforated by three loop-holes. Tradition says that Ballyreagh in ancient times belonged to the McIlenrys, and this is borne out by the Ulster Inquisition, which found that Randal, Earl of Antrim, had, by deed dated November, 1621, granted in perpetuity lands in the parishes of Ballyaghran and Ballywillin to James Oge MacIlenry, other O'Cahan of Ballyreagh. The English Deputy, Sir John Perrott, writing from Dunluce on 17th September, 1584, says: "I have taken Dunferte, the ward being fled, likewise also another pyle in Portrush." This was the castle on Crannagh Hill, and both were destroyed by him.

After a great storm in the year 1827, which swept away the sand on the south side of Causeway Street, the remains of an ancient town of considerable dimensions were exposed to view, showing the foundations of the houses and some of the old hearthstones. There were found domestic utensils, moose deer horns, and several other things of great curiosity. About the year 1886, after another storm, a great blue stone was laid bare, with a flat smooth top, like a table, and a man began to dig about it and dug up a quantity of flint hatchets, flakes, and arrowheads. It seemed to be a place where these flint weapons were manufactured. This ground is now covered by the Kelly Memorial School; and it is strange to say that on this same spot there was a hill forty feet above the level of the street, about seventy years ago. It was quite flat on the top, and about forty steps each way. It served the women to bleach their clothes upon.

On May 10th, 1857 (it fell upon a Sunday), Downhill Castle was partly destroyed by fire, and Mr. Adams, then a little boy, remembers being upon this hill with most of the Springhill people looking at the fire. This hill was all sand, and, owing to storms and the farmers drawing it away and taking it for building purposes, it has all disappeared. At the time Downhill was burned there was neither Eglinton Terrace nor station-house where they now stand, and nothing to mar the view from the westward. Another row of houses (about twelve) stood on the north-east side of Causeway Street on the ground now called Strandmore. They were very old houses, and were all thrown down about the year 1850. They had been mostly inhabited by fishermen and their families.

THE SKERRIES

There is a long range of islands outside of Portrush called the Skerries, nearly a mile and a half long, running from west to east. They are about seventeen in number, but only four on which there is any vegetation-the Small Skerry, the Winkle Isle, the Castle Isle, and Large Skerry. The westernmost island is called West Island, and the easternmost Island Dhu. On the south side of the largest of these islands, and about the middle of it, is good shelter and anchorage in about six fathoms of water. The area of the entire group is about 24 acres. In the year 1315, when Edward Bruce came to Ireland to be crowned king of it, he encamped beside Coleraine, and was attacked by the Earl of Ulster and reduced to great straits; but there was a famous Scottish pirate named Tavish Dhu, who at that time frequented this coast, and often came to anchor at the Skerries. He captured four English vessels which were coming with provisions and other supplies to the English at Coleraine. He sailed up the River Bann with them and gave them to Bruce. Tavish Dhu, sometime after this, came back to the Skerry Roads with his ships and died; and there is an old tradition that he is buried in the Skerries, but where the exact spot is no one can tell.

It is not far from these islands, near the Causeway headland, that the "Gerona," a gigantic galley, impelled by oars, of the Spanish Armada was wrecked. its commander was Alonzo de Lyra, who, says Froude, was so celebrated personally, and had so many attractions combined in him of birth, learning, and distinguished services that of the fathers of the high-born youths who had volunteered to accompany the Armada, most of them had committed their sons to De Lyra's special care. In this galley, to the number of 300, they sailed away from Killybegs, hoping to reach the Scottish coast, where they would be beyond the power of the Lord Deputy of Ireland, who put to death every Spanish soldier and sailor which shipwreck threw into his hands. A violent storm, however, drove the unwieldy "Gerona" on the Causeway headland, and 260 bodies of the flower of the Spanish nobility were washed into the little creek, ever since known as Port-na-Spaniagh.

We are not told by the State Papers how much, if any, of the treasure or ordnance the Government obtained, but the sons of Sorley Boy placed some of the cannon on their fortress of Dunluce Castle; and to this day two exceedingly strong iron chests which had been obtained from the "Gerona" are preserved in Glenarm Castle.

THE WAR HOLLOW

The part of the golf links of the Royal Portrush Golf Club known as "The War Hollow" is said to have been the scene of an ancient battle between the chieftains of the Route and Magnus Barefoot, King of Norway. Magnus became king in 1093, and soon afterwards led an expedition to the south with some of the finest men of his country, taking the Orkneys on his way; then he overran the Hebrides, or Western Isles of Scotland. He even spared not the Holy Isle of Iona, but robbed it and put many of the monks to death. About 1102 he landed in Ulster, on the Antrim coast, and anchored in the shelter of the Skerries Isles, a few miles west of the Giant's Causeway. Men were sent on shore to seize cattle from the Irish pasture grounds of Dalriada and Arachty O'Cahan.

They first surprised Dunluce Castle, and made the chief promise to give them 300 cows within three days. They then marched south-west in search of more plunder, and on the third morning Magnus with his great earls went on shore to meet his men with their plunder.

At this time he was in his fortieth year, and in the prime of life. At night O'Flinn, then the Lord of Dunluce, lit a great fire on the top of Mullahanturk, a small hill on the south-east side of the castle, and it was soon answered from the top of Croaghmore, beyond the bush river, and from Croaghmore it was seen east from Ballycastle to Armoy, and as far south as Loughgiel to the foot of Knocklayd, and all the fighting men of North Dalriada were assembled around Dunluce next morning. It seems these robbers had taken a great deal of booty and cattle from beyond the Bann. The historian says the Norsemen had great difficulty in bringing the cattle to the sea-shore, for at that time the country between Coleraine and the sea was covered with woods and bogs, and was very soft for driving cattle.

It was a bright morning, the 24th of August. The Norsemen laboured hard all morning to get the cattle through the bog; at length they reached an eminence of solid ground where they had a good sea view. They saw to eastward a black moving mass, and they thought it was the promised herd of cattle, but it disappeared again, and seeing no signs of hostility they resumed their march for the sea-shore. At length, coming to a plain near the sea, opposite where their ships lay, the Irish burst upon them from behind a number of small sandhills with a wild "farrach" or battle-cry, and shortly afterwards, coming behind them from the south, they were set upon by a body of the Kinel Owen from Culrath and beyond the Bann, who had followed them to regain the cattle and goods which these robbers had taken.

When Magnus saw he was going to be pressed hard, he called to his general, Evinder Olborg, to sound the trumpet and call all his warriors to the royal standard. But it was not easy to do this, for before they could be gathered together multitudes fell by the overwhelming onslaught of the Irish; and at last, gathering as near as their king as they could get, they made a good stand. Magnus continued the fight with great valour, and exposed himself in the thickest of it. A kern, or one of the third-class Irish soldiers, ran his skeen or dagger through one of Magnus's thighs and left it there. Magnus drew it out and continued the fight, and did not seem to mind it, until a gallowglass attacked him singlehanded. A furious combat ensued between these two warriors, till at length the Irishman, with a wild sweep of his broadsword nearly severed the head from Magnus's body.

His body was taken on board the ships by his son Sigurd, and historians say it was taken to Iona and buried there, as at this time it was said he had turned Christian, if not in practice, at least in name. After his death his son Sigurd brought home the ships to Norway, and this part of Ireland was not troubled by these robbers until the time that Hacon Jarl, Magnus's brother's son, took Dunseverick Castle by stratagem.

THE WHITE ROCKS

Close to the east side of the town is a beautiful strand about two miles long, at the eastern end of which is a long stretch of white limestone rocks, interspersed with caves, twenty-seven in number, some of which stretch under the road leading to the Causeway. Two of these are on the west side of the little stream which runs across the strand. They are called the Smugglers' Caves. It is sometimes difficult to get into the second apartment of the first, as the sand accumulates at the mouth. This inner chamber is capable of holding a number of people. Tradition says that this cave has been used by the smugglers for storing both whiskey and tobacco, which was brought sometimes from Inishowen and deposited here until an opportunity served to take it to a market in Coleraine or some other place. Opposite this cave, on the east side of the stream, is the Wishing Arch, a curious natural arch of white limestone, forty feet high. East of this arch are two more caves, one named the Brock cave and the other the Piper's Cave. An oki tradition says that a piper and his

The White Rocks.

dog went into this cave, and that the dog came out at Dunmull, but the piper never was seen again.

The next place of note is Long Gilbert, where the limestone is quarried. There is a bridge over the sea side of it. It is said to be the mark of an extinct volcano. It got its name from a man of weak intellect named Gilbert MacLoughlin, who fell over it and was killed. At the time Lord Antrim lived in Ballymagarry this man was called Lord Antrim's fool. He was about seven feet high, and never wore shoes. He carried the earl's letters and could run nearly as fast as a horse. He was always ready to start with the hounds when they were going out, and when a fox was started he was always amongst the dogs, and had many narrow escapes of being torn to pieces. One day when the fox was started he was there as usual, and joined in the hunt. The fox made for his den, which was on the precipice, and he managed to get into it; but Gilbert and some of the dogs were not able to stop themselves, and went over the cliff, which is over one hundred feet high at this place. So it has got the name of Long Gilbert ever since. The next place of note is a round hole, like the mouth of a cauldron or pot, on the sea side of the road not far east of Long Gilbert. It has an opening at the bottom into which the sea rages. It is about 70 feet deep, and is called "The

Priest's Hole." In fine weather a boat can go into it from the sea. In the year 1641 a great many Protestants were killed, and a band of them, when escaping to the shore to try to get off to Scotland, were overtaken at a place called Loughlynch. A priest who was blamed for being with the Roman Catholic party was caught near Ballymagarry and thrown into the hole; but after this unfortunate act it was found out that it was not the priest but another man with whom he had exchanged his clothes.

DUNMULL HILL

This hill is situated about two miles south of Portrush, and is the highest in the parish of Dunluce, commanding a magnificent view of the country around. It was said to be a place of Druidical worship in early times. A circle of large stones round the hill is supposed to be an ancient burying-place. A famous stone chair, now lying on the west corner of the hill, is called the Witches' Cradle. In very early times a strong circular fort was built on the summit by the O'Flynns, which in later times was said to have been occupied by one of the Macnaghtens of Benvarden. Before the rebellion of 1641 he retreated to this stronghold with eighty followers, partly Episcopalians, partly Roman Catholics. General Munro surprised them on the hill, and did not spare one of them alive. A farmer named Mr. Todd, who lived to the age of 105, and died about the year 1870, got a great deal of information concerning these times from his father, who also died at an advanced age; he in his turn heard the story of the massacre from his grandfather, who was a young man in 1641, reared, near Ballywillin old church, and who remembered the massacre of Dunmull and the destruction of the fort and the old church of Ballywillin by General Munro.

GLENMANUS

Glenmanus, just outside Portrush, is a very ancient village in the parish of Ballywillin, its former name being Carrig-ard-duth

Varran (the high black rock). This name was, however, changed to Glenmanus in 1642, when it became the property of a wealthy Irish merchant of Coleraine named MacManus. The story is as follows:-MacManus, hearing that General Munro was coming to the relief of Coleraine (then occupied by the Irish), and also hearing that Munro's soldiers were short of boots, had a great many shoes made, and took them in cartloads to Munro, whom he had met at the River Bann. The general was much gratified at the business tact of MacManus, and a short time afterwards MacHenry (O'Cahan) was taken prisoner, his tenants dispersed, and his castle of Dunfert destroyed; only a small piece of the south wall being left standing, which is six feet deep, with loopholes towards the land. McHenry's lands, which were considerable, were confiscated by the English and given to MacManus, and parcelled out to Munro's Scottish soldiers, whose descendants still hold much of the parish. The ruins of Dunfert Castle, which is close to Portrush on the road to Portstewart, stand on a solitary rock facing the Atlantic.

Since those days the small fishing village of yesterday has blossomed into the fashionable watering-place of to-day, visited with delight by the people of many countries. Its bright, healthy streets, swept by the Atlantic breezes; its handsome shops, hotels, and restaurants; its royal golf links, bathing places, promenades, tennis courts, and bowling greens; above all, the grandeur of the land and sea view from Ramore Hill, combine to give Portrush high rank among Irish watering-places.

Dunluce Castle

THE grey ruins of Dunluce, standing on an isolated rock washed by the eternal surge of the Atlantic, are the remains of the castle rebuilt in 1590 by Sir James MacDonnell, son of Sorley Boy, who captured the castle from the MacQuillins, an ancient Norman family of royal descent. Tradition says that, 1,000 years ago, an Irish chieftain named McKeown built the original castle to awe the Danes and the Caledonians, as well as his neighbours. The castle was attacked in the twelfth century by John De Courcy, an Anglo-Norman earl, who, having taken Dunseverick Castle, besieged Dunluce and gained a temporary victory over O'Flinn. Shortly after, O'Flinn completely defeated De Courcy, who is said to have returned to Dublin covered with wounds, and with only eleven followers.

In the thirteenth century Dunluce was besieged by Thomas De Galloway at the head of an English army, and the O'Flinns were driven out. It was in the fourteenth century that the MacQuillins took possession of the castle. In the year 1583 a dispute arose between Sorley Boy MacDonnell and the MacQuillins, and a battle was fought on a plain near Bun-na-Mairgie old church, about half a mile east of Ballycastle. It was fought with fury on both sides, but resulted in the complete defeat of the Mac Quillins. Hugh MacPhelim O'Neill, son of O'Neill of Clanaboye, was slain in the battle, with all the MacQuillin leaders except one-namely, Rory Oge, who lived in Galgorm Castle, near Ballymena.

The MacQuillins were never able after this to muster a fighting force again. The last of them of any note lived in the parish of Dunluce, and was invited to a friendly party, or what would now be called a picnic, at a place called Winehill, about one mile south-east of Bushmills, by the MacDonnells, who also invited the O'Cahans. It was so planned that a MacQuillin was to sit on the left side of a MacDonnell and an O'Cahan. They had all eaten and drunk, and were seeming in the best of friendship, when, at a given signal, each one who sat beside a MacQuillin plunged his dagger into his heart. This foul plot succeeded, and ended the power of the MacQuillins in the Route.

In the days of their prosperity, Mr. McSparran tells the story of their quarrel with O'Donnell. Daniel MacQuillin had formed an alliance with the O'Neills of Clanaboye, and they became fast friends. A rupture having occurred between O'Neill and O'Donnell, MacQuillin espoused the cause of his neighbour, and was implicated in the quarrel. As O'Donnell sat one night surrounded by his kinsmen, his clansmen, and gallowglasses, drinking to the memory of heroes of long ago, two aged minstrels stood behind him, their grey beards hanging down to their girdle, and each clothed with a robe of six different colours-a dignity next to that of an Irish king. "Daniel MacQuillin of Dunluce," said O'Donnell, "has joined the forces of O'Neill of Clanaboye. Does he think that the streams of the Foyle or the Bann will save him?" Turning to the two bards, he told them they must go and inform Daniel MacQuillin that if he would not withdraw his alliance from O'Neill and send his sons as hostages he would pay him a visit in a few days, and maybe an unpleasant one for him. The following day the two revered sages set out for Dunluce Castle, each bearing his harp as an

Dunluce Castle

emblem of his national functions, and arrayed in a robe of six-fold colours. In due time the bards arrived at the castle. It was a festive night with great MacQuillin, who had his friends, the O'Neills of Clanaboye, surrounded by their gallowglasses and kerns, with their bards and senechals playing in concert. A storm burst from the north, driving the sea in wild commotion on the rock which supported the castle. MacQuillin's only daughter entered. She knew Laura O'Donnell, a lady of her own age, educated at the same convent. Laura came sometimes to stay as a guest at Dunluce, and a tender feeling sprang up between her and Finn MacQuillin, the elder brother. The minstrels delivered their message, but Daniel MacQuillin would not give up his alliance with the O'Neills, though he did not wish to quarrel, but to reconcile them. The ministrels then left for Tyrconnell and gave MacQuillm's answer. Laura and her brother urged their father not to quarrel with MacQuillin, but he would not consent, though he agreed to make only a raid and seize the castle of MacQuillin.

The next evening saw him with his friends marching with hostile minds against the peaceable inhabitants of the Route.

Unhappy Laura and the two bards were forced to go with them. The light armed kerns were despatched to the Bann to seize as many boats as they could, and also the boatmen, lest an alarm should be given. This being done, they crossed the Bann in safety. O'Donnell, having posted a strong guard on the ferry, and sending out his men in small detachments, remained in the centre of the county, giving orders to sweep it of horses, cows, and sheep as far as they went; sparing neither the infirm, the orphan, nor the widow, MacQuillin had been at some distance from home, but soon heard the news. The war trumpet was sounded. The great flag bearing the arms of MacQuillin was unfurled, and that night they raised the war-cry on the banks of the Bann.

When young Garry MacQuillin came to the water's edge, being foremost, he saw the boats were all bound fast on the other side, and the boatmen tied with their hands behind their backs so that they were unable to assist them. He, however, spurred his horse with fury into the river, and the faithful animal bore him to the other side; then dismounting, he untied the ferrymen, and the army crossed the river. It was customary, or rather one of the feudal laws prevailing; in those days, that the enemy who could forcibly take the property of another past three crosses situated at a mentioned distance from each other, then became the lawful possessor of it. O'Donnell had placed one cross at the Bann side, another somewhere in a central direction, the last beyond the old church at Drumachose, Limavady. At this cross, defended by a strong guard, he had ordered his lovely daughter Laura to remain, in order that the troops might be more incited to reach the goal.

All day the fight was fierce, and many fell, but it was clear the victory was undecided when evening came. Owen Roe O'Donnell ordered his son to march to the old cemetery of Drumachose and fortify it for their night's encampment, also to escort his sister thither with her maids to fit up a place for the wounded.

Finn MacQuillin strolled out in the calm evening, armed with his broadsword. He made his way to the graveyard, and hearing a heavy sigh as of one in distress, he turned round and saw it was Laura O'Donnell. She burst into a flood of tears, and gently leaned her head on his shoulder. Taking off his cloak he wrapped it round her. As voices were heard near at hand they parted, and Laura's little dog, Dun, called after Dunluce, followed Finn and never left him.

Next day the battle was renewed more fiercely than ever. The two lines closed from one extremity to the other, barricading the front of each with heaps of slain. Poor Laura was left with her maids, and was filled with grief and terror. Finn MacQuillin's white plume, made for him by Laura and his sister, was seen by her all through the fight.

Cahir Roe O'Doherty was a man of more than ordinary stature, and hoping to win the favour of Laura by his prowess in the fight attacked Finn fiercely; the result was the white plume of Finn MacQuillin, together with himself and a bloody sword broken in two, lay prostrate beneath the victor. Little Dun, howing piteously, made his way to the church, and not finding his mistress there, crossed the little brook to the place where she sat with her maids, who, seeing him, drooping and crouching at her feet, knew that all was not well. She did not remain long in suspense. She saw men approaching with the dead body of a soldier to this place, being the goal of victory. It was the body of Finn MacQuillin, his eyes closed, and his white plume dragging in the mud. She rose to meet him with a wild and unsettled look in her eyes. Then, hanging over him for some moments, with her white hands clasped together, bearing in her countenance despair, pity, and inconsolable grief, she stretched herself by his side, with her cheek to his, and drawing her veil over their faces, she seemed to sink into a profound rest, from which her maids did not wish to wake her for a time; but when they ventured silently to withdraw the veil, alas! the spirit of Laura had fled to meet that of her lover in a brighter region.

Meanwhile in other parts of the field the contest had gone in favour of the MacQuillins till a parley was granted for the burial of the dead. The first care of Daniel MacQuillin and his sons was to go in search of the body of Finn, which they found exactly in the place where it was first laid, with Laura O'Donnell at his side, pale and lifeless. Tears stood in the eyes of all as they gathered around. Having laid them on their bier, they inarched forward slowly, the pipers playing a plaintive air, the three MacQuillins and Owen Roe O'Donnell walking before, and Laura's maids behind, weeping as they went. They laid them gently in the same grave. The three brave sons of Owen Roe O'Donnell, who fell in the fight, were interred opposite their sister's tomb, while the father, now childless, returned home to spend the remainder of his days in solitude and woe.

The cattle that evening turned their heads homewards pursuing the same path by which they came, and lowing for their heath-clad hills around Dunluce. she clans of Tyrconnell also marched off the same evening, leaving many of their friends on the bloody field of Cortmore-the oaks of Drenagh Wood and the old church of Drumachose witnesses to a hard contested struggle.

The old castle of Dunluce passed into the hands of the MacDonnells, and was the residence of Lord Antrim till the rebellion of 1641. Soon after, a portion of the castle having fallen into the sea on a wild December night, Lady Antrim left the castle. After a time the roof fell in, and the place has remained a ruin ever since. There were originally five towers; there are only two remaining - Macuihn's Tower on the east side, which contains the remains of a staircase; and a smaller tower seawards, called Mave Roe's Tower; so called after Mave Roe, supposed by some to have been a relative of the MacQuillins, and by others, their banshee, or fairy spirit, whose wail, they say, is still heard above the winter's storm, and who keeps the apartment scrupulously clean, expecting the return of the former owners.

In the churchyard of Dunluce lie the bodies of many of the Spanish sailors wrecked in the "Gerona" in 1588 after the defeat of the Armada, most of them scions of the noblest families of Castille.

BUSHMILLS

THE ancient name of Bushmills, it is stated in "The MacDonnells of Antrim," was Portcammon. It received its present name in 1633 when Sir Randal MacDonnell gave the lease of a mill to Matthew Logan, now called the Walk Mill, with five acres of land thereto. This part of the town was where the church now stands. The following incidents are related in the "Book of Leinster":-

"Now about the time of Christ there dwelt at Ballaghmore a beautiful warrior champion, the chief of the clan. He wore a fine blue-bordered shirt, with carved and interlaced clasps of bronze, and buttons of burnished gold on his breast; above this he wore a coat of most beautiful colours. This was Amergin, the bard of the River Bush, in the north of Dalriada. He was master of his craft, so that there was none better than him, either before or after his day. To him was born a son, named Amergin. This child was fourteen years old before he spoke, but on one occasion when another bard who lived near, called Athern, sent his gillie an errand to the smith, the gillie was saluted by the dumb child twice. When the father of the child heard this, he was afraid this poet would kill the boy if he got an opportunity. He therefore made a likeness of his son, and dressed it in his clothes, and laid it down on the bank of the river Bush in the twilight, as if asleep, and when the other poet came to take his usual walk in the evening, and came upon the boy asleep, as he thought, he struck him three great blows with a club on the head and walked away, thinking he had killed him. But when he found the boy was not dead, nor anything the worse, he repented of what he had done, and matters were smoothed up between them, Athern then took the boy and made him a famous poet. He was chief of all the poets of Dalriada, and afterwards became chief poet of Connor McNeese, King of Ulster, who reigned at this time. This happened early in the first century, and at the time Christ was upon earth. It is also recorded that there was abundance of cattle and corn and fruit in this part of Erin at this time, and that there was no stormy weather, thunder nor lightning, and the wind did not take a hair off the cattle from October to May."

The river Bush is called in "The Book of Leinster" the Inbher Bosha Bruchta Scrobha-the river of the bursting torrents. It appears that a large tract of land on the east side of the river Bush belonged to a gentleman named Donal Oge MacDuff, and his place of abode was called Clougher. The name MacDuff, is now changed to McAfee, which is very common around the locality yet. It is said they are descendants of Colla Na Cappa MacDonnell, or Colla of the Black Mare, who lived in Dunluce after the rebellion of 1641. Many of these people Anglicised their name to Black-some say when they turned Protestants.

THE GIANT'S CAUSEWAY

THE Giant's Causeway, probably the most extensive and curious assemblage of basaltic columns in the world, is situated between Port-na-Grange and Port Noffer, and derives its name from a popular tradition that it was erected by giants as the commencement of a causeway across the ocean to Scotland. The Causeway is divided into three unequal parts. The Little or Western Causeway is 386 feet long, but only 16 feet high, and is separated from the central compartment by an enormous whin dyke, extending from the cliff to the sea. The middle section, which is the shortest, contains a magnificent group of lofty pillars, called "The Honeycomb," and is also bounded on the east by a whin dyke. Beyond this is the Grand Causeway, which is 706 feet long by 109 wide in the middle. In that part of this compartment which is called "The Loom," it attains an elevation of 34 feet, from which it diminishes in height gradually as it approaches the sea, into which it enters for some distance beyond low-water mark. In the western and central compartments all the columns are perpendicular, but in the Grand Causeway they are vertical towards the east-inclining eastward as they approach the sea, and westward near the base of the cliff.

Giant's Causeway

The three divisions of the Causeway comprise 37,426 distinct and perfect columns, besides many that are broken and scattered about in its vicinity. The columns consist of prisms of equal dimensions through their whole height, which ranges from 15 to 36 feet, with diameter of from 15 to 28 inches, and varying in their number of sides from three to nine, although the greater number are pentagons and hexagons. Each of the pillars is perfectly distinct, and almost invariably differs in size, number of sides, and points of articulation from the adjacent columns, to which, however, it is so close that not even water can pass between them.

Almost every column is composed of several pieces, the joints of which are articulated with the greatest exactness, and in a strictly horizontal direction; generally the upper part of the section is concave and the lower convex, but this arrangement is sometimes reversed. In a few of the columns no joints are visible; in others, three, four, or more may be traced. In the west side of the Causeway, just below the "Giant's Punchbowl," a well of the purest water will be found springing from between the fine interstices of the pillars, and by the removal of one of the joints a beautiful little hexagonal basin is formed, from which a draught of icy water can be procured in the hottest day in summer.

The basalt of which these columns are composed is of a very dark colour, approaching to black; its weight is three times as great as that of water. Nearly 300 yards east of the Causeway is " The Giant's Organ," about 120 feet long, consisting of 60 columns, of which those in the centre are 40 feet high, but those on the side are lower. At the eastern extremity of Port Noffer are four lofty and massive basaltic columns, rising to a height of 315 feet; they are hexagonal and jointed, and from their height and isolated position are called "The Chimney Pots." Near these is "The Theatre," consisting of three distinct colonnades.

The most picturesque cliff is Pleaskin, which rises from the sea in a gentle acclivity for more than 300 feet, and then ascends perpendicularly 70 feet to its summit. This headland, which is unrivalled for beauty of arrangement and variety of colouring, is seen to most advantage from the sea, from which also some of the grandest views of the Causeway and its adjacent scenery are obtained. Fossil wood, as black and compact as coal, and fossil oysters and mussels are found in the limestone rock that forms the substratum of the Causeway and its neighbouring promontories; and large opals, chalcedony, and agates are collected here. Specimens of these fossils and minerals, and two wooden models of the Causeway are in the Museum of Trinity College, Dublin.

Sir Humphrey Davy often visited the Causeway when fishing in the Bush, and talked with the guides and gave them much information. John Whitehurst, who wrote in 1786 a treatise on the "Original state and formation of the Earth," has written with much accuracy on the Causeway. Of its origin he says: " Some doubts may arise, since no visible crater nor the least vestige of an extinct volcano is now remaining from which such enormous torrents flowed, so as to cover so large an area; but " he adds, "whoever attentively considers these remarkable cliffs will, I presume, soon discover sufficient cause to conclude that the crater from which the melted matter flowed, together with an immense tract to the north, has been absolutely sunk and swallowed up at some remote period of time, and now lies at the bottom of the Atlantic Ocean."

The Rev. William Hamilton, in his letters on the coast of Antrim, and Dr. Richardson of Clonfeckle, have both written with much care, and recorded observations of great value worthy of attention. The caves are interesting. Portcoan is one of the finest. Boats can penetrate it for 130 yards. It is 40 feet high and has a fine entrance. It is probable that seals once made this cave their abode. A little to the west of Portcoan is Runkerry cave. It is larger than its neighbours, being 700 feet long. The entrance is 26 feet in breadth and in the form of a Gothic arch, and the roof of the cave is 60 feet high. The strange roaring of the water in the interior gives a weirdness to the cave, and there is a sensation of being lifted up towards its roof-both phenomena being produced by the compressed air of the interior; there is, however, no danger. This cave also has fine echoes. The most striking feature, perhaps, of the surface of County Antrim are its mountains, which stretch in a regular outline from the southern to the northern extremities, terminating on the shore in abrupt and almost perpendicular declivities. They attain their greatest elevation near the coast, and have a gradual descent inland, so that many of the principal streams have their sources near the sea, and run directly thence towards Lough Neagh. These mountains are computed to occupy about one-third of the superficial area of the county. The most remarkable range of cliffs are those of perpendicular basaltic columns, which extend for many miles and form a coast of surpassing magnificence washed by the eternal swish of the Atlantic waves. Of these cliffs the most striking are the Giant's Causeway and Fair Head, which project several hundred feet into the sea.

Dunseverick Castle

Dunseverick Castle stands on an isolated rock nearly surrounded by the sea, in a small bay about one mile and a half east of the Giant's Causeway. Tradition says it was the residence of Conal Cearnach, the famous Ulster hero in the Ultonian literature, and champion of the Red Branch Knights. It used to be told by the Glens of Antrim folk that Conal Cearnach during his wanderings abroad was present at the Crucifixion, and that he was the first to bring the tidings to Ireland. Dunseverick Castle was in later days the family residence of an old Irish sept called O'Cahan, a branch of the Kind Owen, from a very early date. This family held it until the rebellion of 1641, when its chief, Gilladuff O'Cahan, was taken by General Munro and hanged at Carrickfergus some years after the rebellion was ended. Munro destroyed all the castles around the coast except Dunluce, which he garrisoned with English soldiers. Dunseverick was all thrown down except a piece of wall at the entrance six feet thick, which his men were not able to remove.

The most curious thing about this castle is a well on the north side, about three yards from the edge of the cliff, which is over one hundred feet above the sea This well, it is said, never goes dry. It is called Tubber Phadrick, or St. Patrick's Well. It was at one time considered one of the holy wells of Ireland. St. Patrick, it appears, visited Dunseverick on several occasions on his travels through the North. A great many people brought their children to him to be baptized, and amongst them St. Olcan, who afterwards became Bishop of Armoy, now a small town in North Antrim. A large stone stood beside the well, called St. Patrick's Rock, but it was tumbled into the well by the soldiers of General Munro. The saint used to sit on this stone when he came to Dunseverick.

Dunseverick Castle

Colgan, in an interesting note on the antiquity of Dunseverick, says: "Dunseverick is a maritime and remotely ancient fortress in the territory of Dalriada, which derives its name from Sovaric, the son of Eberic, the first founder of the fortress, about the year of the world 3668 A.M., as may be learned from the four Masters in their 'Annals,' and from Dr. Keating in his catalogue of Irish kings. In the year A.D. 870 Dunseverick Castle was stormed (by whom it is not said), a thing which never happened before. Again, it was plundered by Mave, Queen of Connaught, but the date is uncertain. She came into Ulster with a great host of warriors from Connaught, and amongst other places she surprised Dunseverick, and drove off a great herd of cattle, and amongst them was the famous ' tarif bhan ' (white bull) of Cuailgne. This started a long and bloody war between Ulster and Connaught."

An extract from an old English manuscript gives an account of another disaster to Dunseverick Castle in the twelfth century: " Many hundred years ago there stood on Erin's northern coast a stately castle called Dunseverick. It was inhabited by a noble family of the Kinel Owen. It was thronged with gallowglasses and kerns and attendants of the powerful chief who dwelt in it. No foe had dared to annoy it for many years. At last news reached Ireland that King Baldwin of Flanders and Godfrey De Bouillon were enrolling a body of young men to join the Crusaders. The young heir of Dunseverick got his father's consent, and got enrolled under the banner of the Cross. Many of the sons of the northern chiefs accompanied young Turlough of Dunseverick. Ere long these young Irishmen proved by deeds that they were second to none in Europe for warlike achievements and feats of arms, and the fame of Ireland was spread abroad as the island of warriors and scholars. When Antioch was besieged young Turlough was among the first to mount the walls, and ten months later, when the Holy City was taken, Turlough was found in the thick of the fight till the last of the Turks was slain and the streets were running with blood. Then Godfrey De Bouillon was crowned King of Jerusalem, with the title of Protector of the Holy Sepulchre. Most of the Crusaders then returned home, and with them was Turlough of Dunseverick. But in his absence a terrible calamity had befallen his family and his home. The Norwegians had arrived with a great fleet of ships, and landed some place not far from Dunseverick, and marched at night-time to the castle and gained admission to it through stratagem, and massacred all the inhabitants of the castle. The only one of the family who was spared was the young Lady O'Cahan, sister of Turlough. This beautiful young girl, with her dark brown hair and blue eyes, won the heart of the Norseman, and he determined to spare her for himself; but she was deaf to all entreaties until he would become a Christian. To this he soon consented, to accomplish his purpose. One of the monks of Camus, on the River Bann, was sent for to prepare and baptize him, and the wedding-day was fixed. A great assembly was gathered to witness the ceremony of the baptism and marriage of the Norseman and the young Irish lady. At length the penitent advanced to the middle of the great hall to make a public confession of his crimes, and then the priest advanced with mitre, stole, and crozier in hand and solemnly addressed the kneeling penitent. A tall, dark, powerful-looking figure appeared amongst the crowd, clad in a great shaggy cloak of native Irish fashion, and pushed through the throng until he came to the middle of the hall, where the priest and penitent were. This was the young Crusader from Palestine, Turlough of Dunseverick.   In   the deadly   conflict   that   ensued between Turlough and the Norseman the castle caught fire, and the horror-stricken assemblage fled down the steep incline that led to the causeway below, which connected the rock that the castle stood upon to the mainland. A wild cry went up from the crowd below when they heard that the young bride rushed out from the burning castle and flung herself from the cliff on the north side into the sea. Thus was Dunsevenck left in ruins once more.

"And the villagers of olden times oft heard the wailing cry
Of the Norseman and brave young Turlough when waves were running high,
And old Dunseveric, gaunt and bare, has no sadder tale of woe
Recorded in its annals of the years of long ago."

These events are recorded by antiquarian writers, from whom I quote, on the authority of ancient manuscripts, and the tales they tell are historic facts of the past mingled with legend. How long Dunseverick lay waste after this calamity is not known, but it is certain the castle was rebuilt and taken possession of by another branch of the same family, and was finally captured and destroyed shortly after the rising of 1641 by the ruthless General Munro.

BALLINTOY AND CARRICK-A-REDE

OF all the families that came over to North Antrim from the neighbouring shores of Scotland, none developed or spread so much as the Stewarts of Ballintoy. The original residence of the family was an old castle on Altmore, or the Deerpark, on the high land south of Ballintoy; but they afterwards removed to the Castle of Ballintoy, once a residence of the MacQuillins, the site of which is now occupied by a cluster of farmhouses. It was in 1625 that Archibald Stewart received a grant from Randal MacDonnell, first Earl of Antrim, of the districts known as Ballylough and Ballintoy, each containing four quarters of land, Irish measure, for the yearly rent of £9 sterling. This grant included Sheep Island and the other little island of Portcampbell, which were of no use for anything but for the seaweed that grew upon them, being used for making kelp. The church, which stands near the site of the old castle, was rebuilt in 1812 by the Rev. Robert Traill.

The head of the Stewart family was very frequently rector of the parish, and on an old bell of the church there is the following inscription: " Archibald Stewart gave me: Charles, his son, recast me, anno 1686; and Archibald, the son of Charles, recast and augmented me, anno 1718. "The Rev. Robert Traill rebuilt the church. The old Rectory was standing in the days of the Armada, but was rebuilt during the Incumbency of Dr. Carter. It stands on the hill above Ballintoy called "Mount Druid," from the fact that a cromlech stands in the grounds. Round the cromlech the stone circle is still complete.

The far-famed swinging bridge of Carrick-a-rede (carrig-a-riada, the "intercepting rock"), which stands in the way of the course of the salmon along the coast, is a great object of interest and curiosity to the visitors and tourists, who in large numbers frequent this place in summer, which is about a mile from the village. The span is about 60 feet, and the height above the water-level 90 feet. Across this chasm two ropes are strung with transverse connections; two slight ropes, elevated convenient to the hand, run parallel with the footway as a guide in crossing. The width of the bridge is about two and a half feet. Visitors are cautioned against the danger of crossing, but the fishermen carry loads of salmon across without the least fear. In stormy weather, however, even these hardy men are daunted, and would not set foot on it. Until recently there was only one slight rope elevated to the hand.

About half a mile from Dunseverick and about two miles west of Ballintoy is the old church and burying-ground of Templastragh, or, as it was called, the church gobhan tsier, as in ancient times builders of the castles and churches were called by the name of "gobhan tsier" which means a smith, carpenter and mason. There is an old tradition which the people of the neighbourhood tell, that when it was building, what was built in the daytime was thrown down every night, and a light was seen a small distance east of it, unto which the workmen removed, and commenced their work again. This place seemed to please the light which appeared, and the church was not thrown down again. An account of this church is given in "The MacDonnells of Antrim," which says: Templastragh Church was built in the year 648 by St. Gobhan, commonly called Gobhanseir-from gobhan, a smith, and tsier, a carpenter, and he was also a preacher of the Gospel. Rogha and Lassara were sisters of St.

Colman, who was the patron saint of Derrykeighan. They were orphans, and were fostered or brought up by St. Congall of Bangor, County Down. They died in the latter part of the sixth century, and were buried in the Camus graveyard on the west side of the River Bann, not far from Coleraine. The mother of these three orphans was said to be the daughter of Milcho, the chief who bought St. Patrick and kept him as a slave. This chief's residence was beside Slemish Mountain, upon which the saint used to herd sheep and swine. The mountain is not far east of Ballymena.

The old graveyard is situated on a level plain on the top of what is called Rossmore, which has a perpendicular cliff on the north side, next the sea of about one hundred feet. A little to the west of Rossmore cliff is a large cave, which the sea does not enter, called the Skull Cave, where at one time a great number of skulls were found, said to be those of people who had been killed in the rebellion of 1641. The church was dedicated to Saint Lassara and called Templassara, now Templastragh (the Church of St. Lassara).

BALLYCASTLE

BALLYCASTLE, the charming watering-place on the coast of Antrim, has not the stern grandeur of Portrush, but nature has done much to make the whole district beautiful. It abounds with the most varied scenery in mountain, upland, glen, and cliff, and is beautifully wooded almost to the seashore. The golf links, small but sporting, the tennis courts, and bowling greens are gay in the summer months with happy young people, and one cannot wonder that Ballycastle is a cherished spot in the affections of its many visitors.

It has also a history full of interest. It is said to have been from Port Brittas, the old name for Ballycastle Bay, that in A.D. 506 the chiefs Angus and Fergus, with many followers from the Antrim Dalnada, sailed to Scotland, and after a succession of battles to have founded a large colony, which included, besides other territories along the coast of Scotland, the Isles and Cantire. In 1494, after being defeated by King James IV of Scotland, the MacDonnells, followed by their clansmen, the MacNeills, MacAlisters, and MacKays, settled in Antrim. It was from this time that the struggle began between the MacDonnells and MacQuillins for the Antrim Dalriada or Route.

In 1550 Alexander MacDonnell was established at Dunaneeny Castle, where, with Port Brittas at his feet, he commanded the key of the position, as he could bring galleys "go leor" from Cantire and the Isles to help him in his battles. Nine years after this the MacQuillins were defeated and almost exterminated in the Glenshesc Valley by Sorley Boy MacDonnell and his followers, and so it came about that by the end of the sixteenth century the MacDonnells were masters of the situation, and held the Route, the Glens, and Rathlin, with numerous castles.

In ancient times a castle stood on the site of the Boyd Church in the Diamond, and it was from this castle that Ballycastle derived its name. After the MacDonnells had become masters of North Antrim, one of their earliest grants conveyed the lands constituting the Ballycastle estate to Hugh MacNeill That grant is dated 9th November, 1612, and reserves to Sir Randal MacDonnell and his wife, Lady Alice O'Neill, the right of residence, should they wish it, at either or both villages of Dunanynie and Ballycashan (Baile Cashlin, Ballycastle). They availed themselves of this privilege some years afterwards, and built a new castle on the site of the old one which had given the name of Ballycastle to the village. The ordnance MS. states that in 1838 there was, over a back door in the house of Mrs. Blair, on the south side of Main Street, a date stone which had been taken from the ruins of the castle, and on which was an inscription in raised letters, but the only portion of it that could be read was "WRKGS 1625," which was probably the date at which the earl erected the new castle.

He died at Dunluce in 1636, and his wife, the Lady Alice O'Neill, with their two daughters, went to live at Ballycastle. Here she resided, enjoying the rents of her extensive jointure lands, until 1642, when she suddenly found herself in the very centre of the bloody deeds which were committed by both parties at that period of great rebellion. The castle was seized by Scotch troops, and afterwards held by the Cromwellians. The old countess returned to the neighbourhood after the Restoration. One of her letters, written from Bun-na-mairgie, is dated 1661, and in another, written in the same month, she prays her "Dear Cousin, Colonel Robert Stewart, now in Dublin - 'I hope you will strive to get my old dwelling Ballycastle to me again.'" The castle, however, had been too long occupied by soldiers to be reoccupied as a mansion. The eastern gable remained until 1848, when it was removed by an order from the Court of Chancery, lest its fall might occasion loss of life.

After the wars of 1641 Ballycastle was almost entirely deserted. At the end of the century the village occupied only an extent of three acres. About 1736 Mr. Hugh Boyd, son of the rector of Ramoan, secured a lease from the Antrim family, and having obtained £20,000 from Parliament he built a pier for the protection of shipping. He sank coal shafts, established potteries, built smelting-houses and a glass factory, and under his fostering care the village of Ballycastle blossomed into a flourishing town. At the time of his death in 1765 the town had twenty vessels actively employed in trade, but from that period the harbour was permitted to fall into decay. The violence of the tides overthrew the piers, and the harbour was choked with drifted sands.

KINBAN

On the sea coast, on the way to the Causeway, stand the ruins of the castle of Kinban, "The White Head," that guarded the limestone promontory from which it is named. It occupies a bold position over the chasm separating that promontory from the mainland. At present little remains of the fortress except a part of the keep, a portion of the gateway, and fragments of the courtyard and of the walls that once guarded the edges of the cliff. At the base of the headland is Lagna-Sassanach, "the hollow of the English" where it is said an English force once encamped to besiege the castle, but the garrison having sallied out at night, occupied the height above the camp and rolled over the precipices masses of rock with which they crushed the enemy. Tradition says Kinban was built by the MacHenrys, but in the beginning of the reign of Queen Elizabeth it was held by the MacAlisters. In an attack by Captain Piere, of Carrickfergus, three of the MacAlisters who were in rebellion were made prisoners; one of them was hung in chains, and Alister, chief of the clan, made his submission to the English. The MacAlisters after this were forced again into rebellion, but were overpowered and their castle destroyed. It was rebuilt by Coll MacDonnell, who lived in it till 1558; but after the rising of 1641 it was finally destroyed by the ruthless Scotch General-Munro-to whom the destruction of so many stately castles in Antrim is due.

Kinban Castle

DUNANEENY CASTLE

This fortress stands on the summit of a bold promontory that rises to a great height above the sea. Dunaneeny means "the fort of the assembly or fair." The area on which the castle stood is a smooth level, measuring from east to west 60 yards, and from north to south 35 yards. It was surrounded by the sea on all sides except the south, where it was protected by a moat extending from east to west 80 yards, cut chiefly through the solid rock. The highest part of the wall now remaining is only 12.5 feet, and every vestige of the castle which stood within the fortified area has disappeared. Tradition says it was built by the O'Carrols, an old family who resided here many centuries ago. Later, the chieftains of the MacDonnells made this one of their principal strongholds, and from it they could watch their galleys gliding into Port Brittas almost at its base. The castle is notable for being the birthplace of the second Sorley Boy MacDonnell, who was born here in 1505. It was from here, at the head of his kerns and gallowglasses, he led them from victory to victory, till he became master of the whole of the Route. It was here, too, he died, and from here he was carried to his resting-place, the procession making its way through Ballycastle to the Abbey of Bun-na- mairgie, where they laid their gallant chief in a soldier's grave.

The ruins of this ancient church and friary are only a few minutes' walk from Ballycastle. The friary is said to have been built by the MacQuillins, and to have been enlarged by the MacDonnells. Formerly a river ran close to the abbey, but its course was diverted in 1738 by Mr. Boyd, in order that it might help to deepen the inner dock. The church and friary were built of Ballycastle sandstone, filled in with small stones. From the fourteenth or fifteenth century it was occupied by Franciscan friars of the third order. The church suffered considerable damage on 4th January, 1584, when the English of the Pale, under Sir John Perrott, marched to Bun-na-mairgie, where, leaving his cavalry in charge of Sir William Stanley in and around the church, he placed his infantry in the Fort of Ballycastle. Sorley Boy was on his way home with several galleys full of Scots, but his followers, anticipating his arrival, attacked the English troops at Bun-na-mairgie at one o'clock in the morning, and set fire to the roof of the church, which was thatched. The church was full of horses. A severe battle ensued, in which Sir William Stanley was wounded, and Sir John Perrott was forced to withdraw his troops, but took with him St. Columba's cross from the church, which he sent to Sir Francis Walshingham, describing it as Sorley Boy's cross, with a request it should be given to Lady Walshingham. The church was subsequently restored and the friary again reoccupied.

Fair Head

The churchyard of Bun-na-mairgie was the burial place of the MacDonnells. The place, says Rev. George Hill, heaves with the MacDonnell dust. There were those who fell when James MacDonnell slaughtered the MacQuillins in Glenshesc at the battle of Aura. There were those who fell when Shane O'Neill overthrew Sorley MacDonnell and his brother James in 1665 at Glenshesc or Glentow. There were, too, those who fell around Bun-na-mairgie in 1584 when Sorley Boy and his followers repulsed Sir John Perrott and his followers. It is said that during this period heaps of bodies were carried there and left unburied for weeks until an opportunity came.

CATH RIGH AN ULADH
(Castle of the King of Ulster)

There is a beautiful green eminence nearly two miles north-east of Ballycastle and a short distance south of Carey Church. It is said to have been a summer residence of King Connor MacNeasa, the celebrated King of Ulster, who began his reign about twelve years after the birth of Christ. He was called MacNeasa from his mother, Neasa, who was daughter of an Irish chief, and was left a widow in the prime of youth and beauty. At this time Fergus MacRoigh was King of Ulster, and when Connor was seven years old Fergus fell in love with the widow and proposed marriage to her, with a request to name her dowry. The widow consented on condition that the sovereignty of the province should be resigned to her son Connor for one year, in order, as she said, that his children should be called the children of a king. Fergus took counsel with his people, and they advised him to agree to the condition, seeing that the youth would likely be only too glad to get rid of the cares of government long before the year expired.

In this they were mistaken; for when his mother found herself in a position of wealth and influence, she supplied the boy and his tutors with all the money and other wealth that she could lay hold on, to be distributed secretly among the most important and powerful chiefs of the province. She also advised and enabled him to keep up a style of splendour and hospitality such as none of his predecessors had ever done before, so that his court became the resort of all that were brave and dignified, scientific and learned, in the kingdom. The poets extolled him in verse; the druids prophesied his future fame and renown; the ladies loved him for his beauty; the chiefs and warriors looked up to him as the very soul of munificence and chivalry. So that, when the year of office had expired, the Ultonians refused to allow him to hand the kingdom back to Fergus; alleging, among other things, that Fergus appeared willing at any time to barter it and then for the sake of any woman who took his fancy. Fergus did not submit tamely to this breach of covenant. He raised a war against Connor, which was carried on for a long time with vigour; but he was ultimately defeated and forced to an involuntary submission.

Years after, in battle, a brain-ball was flung by Cet, an enemy of Connor, and thrown so that it entered Connor's brow and sank two-thirds into it. He fell with his head to the earth. A physician was brought to Connor-namely, Fingan. "Good!" said Fingan; "if the ball be taken out of thy head thou shalt surely die, and if it is not taken out I could cure thee; but it would be a blemish." Then said the Ultonians: "It is better for us than his death." His head then healed up, and Fingan warned King Connor that he should be cautious; that he should not allow anger to come upon him, that he should not ride upon a horse, neither should be run. And King Connor continued in that doubtful state for the space of seven years, and was incapable of action, and always remained sitting, until he heard that Christ was crucified by the Jews.

There came at that time a great convulsion over creation. The heavens and the earth were shaken by the enormity of the deed that was done-namely, Jesus Christ, the Son of the living God, to be crucified without crime. "What is this?" said Connor to his druid. "What great evil is it which is done on this day?" "It is true, indeed," said the druid, "that Christ, the Son of God, is crucified by the Jews." "That is a great deed," said Connor. "Now," said the druid, "it was on the same day that you were born, that He was born. That is, on the eighth of the calends of January" (though the year was not the same at that time). It was then that Connor believed he was one of the two first men that believed in the Saviour in Erin before the coming of St. Patrick, Moran being the other. "Good, now," said King Connor; "it is a pity that Christ did not apply to a valiant high king which would come in the shape of a champion to do battle for him. Were I there I would kill those who were around my King at the putting of Him to death." And with that he brought down his sword from its place, and he rushed into the woody grove which was convenient, and began to cut down the branches, and what he said was this: that that was the usage he would give them; and from the fury that seized upon him the ball started out of his forehead, and some of his brains came out along with it, and in that hour he died.

Rathlin Island

On the coast of Antrim, just off Ballycastle, lies the island of Rathlin. It is mainly a huge basaltic rock with a precipitous coastline. It contains an area of 4,000 acres, of which 1,000 are sheltered and capable of cultivation, the rest being heather and rock. The approach is at all times dangerous; the tide sets fiercely through the straits which divide the island from the mainland, and when the wind is from the west the Atlantic swell renders it impossible to land. The situation and the difficulty of access had thus long marked Rathlin as a place of refuge for Scotch or Irish fugitives, and, besides its natural strength, it was respected as a sanctuary having been the abode at one time of St. Columba. A mass of broken masonry on a cliff overhanging the sea is a remnant of the castle in which Robert Bruce watched the climbing of the spider.

When Lord Essex, the English Deputy, entered Antrim to attack Sorley Boy MacDonnell, it was to this island that Sorley Boy and the other Scots sent their wives and children, their aged and sick, for safety. Lord Essex, knowing that the refugees were still on the island, sent orders to Colonel John Norris, who was in command at Carrickfergus, to take a company of soldiers with him, cross over to Rathlin, and kill what he could find. The sea, says Froude, to whom I am indebted for this account, was smooth; there was a light and favourable breeze from the east, so that the run up the Antrim coast was rapid and quickly accomplished. Before the alarm could be given, the English had landed close to the ruins of the church which bears St. Columba's name.

Bruce's castle was then standing, and was occupied by a score or two of Scots, who were in charge of the women. Norris had brought cannon with him, so that the weak defences were speedily destroyed, and after a fierce assault, in which several of the garrison were killed, the Scots were obliged to yield at discretion, and every living thing in the place, except the chief and his family, who were probably reserved for ransom, was immediately put to the sword. Two hundred were killed in the castle. It was then discovered that several hundred more, chiefly mothers and their little ones, were hidden in the caves about the shore. There was no pity for them. They were hunted out as if they had been seals or otters, and all destroyed. Sorley Boy and the other chiefs, wrote Essex to Queen Elizabeth, had sent their wives and children into the island, "which be all taken and executed to the number of 600." Sorley Boy himself, he continued, stood upon the mainland of " the Glynnes and saw the taking of the island, and was likely to have run mad for sorrow, tearing and tormenting himself and saying that he there lost all that he ever had."

Such was the tragedy of the 22nd July, 1575. Lord Essex described it as one of the exploits with which he was most satisfied, and Queen Elizabeth, in answer to his letter, bade him tell John Norris, "the executioner of his well-designed enterprise, that she would not be unmindful of his services." Such was the verdict on the massacre in those fierce times, but in more modern days this massacre has left a stain on the memory of Lord Essex that will not soon be obliterated.

THE GLENS OF ANTRIM

THE Glens of Antrim (glynnes-i.e., woods of Antrim) are possessed of scenery unsurpassed anywhere, and it is little wonder that Sorley Boy MacDonnell fought hard with the English of the Pale, and with Essex and his adventurers, to keep and hand them down to his descendants. The glens are nine in number, and open out to the sea at intervals from Glenarm to Ballycastle. They are named Glentow, Glenshesc, Glendun, Glencorp, Glenan, Glenballyemon, Glenariff, Glencoy, and Glenarm, which encloses Glenarm Castle. In the centre is the little village of Cushendall, from which many interesting excursions can be made. The Rev. George Hill says:- "It is admitted even by those who have had opportunities of visiting other lands, that the picturesque beauty of this district is in some respects unrivalled. Each glen is found to possess its own peculiar charms, whilst throughout all the same leading characteristics are apparent."

Glenariff is the most beautiful glen of all, with its many waterfalls and richly wooded scenery. she name is derived from Glynn Aircomb (valley of the numbers, probably referring to the various waterfalls). The glen begins at Parkmore, and the river at one place, at the Ess-na-Leara (fall of the mare), drops from a height of one hundred feet, breaking over a rocky ledge. Soon after the Parkmore or Glenariff river is met by the river Inver, coming up through a charming dell from the south, and then they fall in two silvery sheets of water and spray over the dark basalt into a pool fifty feet below, close to which the visitor may approach. This is the lovely Ess-na-Crub (horse-shoe fall). From this point the united streams flow on to Waterfoot, sinking into quiet and well-earned repose in the sea. The length of the glen is about two miles. There are two other waterfalls in the glen - "The Serpent's Fall" and "The Hermit's Fall." Great facilities for seeing these falls have been made in recent years by the railway company, who have laid down footpaths and picturesque rustic bridges.

The ruins of the old parish church of Ladye may be seen in a little valley near the shore, about a mile north-east of Cushendall. At what time the original buildings fell into ruin cannot now be accurately known, but it was doubtless burned and harried during some of the frequent feuds between the clans of the O'Neill and MacDonnell. Next to Bun-na- margie, Ladye was the favourite burial-place of the MacDonnells, and is still used by the descendants of that ancient clan. The west end of the church is sacred to their dust, and many quaint stones record their name and lineage. On the hill over Cushendun Bay, some three miles from Cushendall, may be seen rude remains of a fort, and some traces of an ancient ecclesiastical building called Cruscrene.

It was here that Shane O'Neill met his death. He arrived with fifty of his followers on Saturday, the last day of May, 1567, after his defeat near Derry, to seek hospitality from Alister MacDonnell and his nephew, Gillespie, who were encamped here. Shane had brought with him as peace offerings the Countess of Argyll and Sorley Boy MacDonnell, who were his prisoners. He was received with kindness, and the old feud between them seemed to be buried in the restoration of Sorley Boy. An alliance was again talked of, and for two days all went well. But on the third evening after supper a quarrel took place, and Shane and most of his followers were stabbed to death. Shane's mangled body was thrown into a pit, but an officer of the nearest garrison, hearing of the massacre, begged to have the head cut off, pickled it, and sent it to the Lord Deputy, who left it to blacken where so many Irish heads had blackened and were still to blacken-over the gate of Dublin Castle. The MacDonnells were more civilised than this English noble in their vengeance. Shane's body, wrapped, "for lack of a better shroud, in a kerne's old shirt," was miserably interred at Glenarm, the home of the MacDonnell chief. The O'Neills besought that the remains of their great chief might rest with his own kin. But the abbot of the monastery answered: "Have you not in your church James MacDonnell, Lord of Antrim and Cantire, who was buried among strangers at Armagh? Then, whilst you continue to tread on the grave of James, Lord of Antrim and Cantire, know ye that we in Glenarm will trample on the dust of your great O'Neill." Yet after Shane's death, the O'Neills and MacDonnells contracted an alliance.

About two miles north-east of Cushendall in a field are to be found a remarkable group of stones Known as "Ossian's grave." It is approached by a by-way from the road leading from Cushendall to Ballymoney by way of the Glenan river. Its position on a mountain spur, looking down two glens and across the Channel to the Scottish coast, is decidedly picturesque. The grouping of the stones is puzzling.

From some points of view, says the official report, they appear a mere jumble, but from the southward it becomes evident that at least eight of them touched an arc of a circle, which would have a diameter of about twenty feet. Nothing seems to be known of their origin. The association of the stones with Ossian - a celebrated Irish warrior bard, who is said to have survived into the Christian period, and to have conversed with St. Patrick - is probably only an example of the characteristic legend which grows up to account for any striking object of which there is no reasonable explanation to the popular mind. It is likely that the monument is commemorative of some chieftain who ruled over the two valleys down which the mountain looks. Its date, like that of the Giant's Ring, is probably many centuries before the Christian era.

A little more than a mile from Cushendall, on a high cliff on the road to Larne, stands the ruin of Red Bay Castle, gaunt and grey, 125 feet above the sea. Of this once proud stronghold nothing remains but crumbling ruins. In the middle of the sixteenth century it was in possession of James MacDonnell, an elder brother of Sorley Boy. In 1561, Piers, the constable of Carrickfergus, sent an officer to Red Bay and complained of Sorley Boy's want of loyalty, but he received very little sympathy from James, and reported that he found the castle being repaired by Scottish workmen, and that James used very evil talk against the Queen (Elizabeth), and said that the Queen of Scotland was rightful heir. At this time Shane O'Neill was on good terms with Queen Elizabeth, and thought he could show his zeal in her cause in no better way than by driving out the interfering Scots, who were settled in such swarms along the Antrim coast.

Red Bay Castle.

Accordingly, in 1565, he marched north, and into the Glens, and attacked Red Bay Castle in the absence of its chief. Signal fires blazed on Torr Head, and James MacDonnell, head of the clan, hastened over from Cantire; but by the time he landed in Red Bay, Shane had taken his castle in the red sandstone cliff, and was on his way towards Ballycastle and the MacDonnell sanctuary at Bunamargy. By the Margy river the whole force of the MacDonnells arrayed itself against him. Three of the MacDonnell brothers went into the fight-one was slain, but James, Lord of Cantire and Antrim, and Sorley Boy, his brother, were taken prisoners. James died in captivity, but two years after the battle Sorley Boy was released. Red Bay Castle was then repaired, and was the scene of many a bloody battle in the long war of the English against Sorley Boy MacDonnell.

GLENARM

FROM Cushendall to Larne is twenty-five miles distant on an excellent and level road, and the view all the way is striking and picturesque. The road runs inland for about a mile from Cushendall, then you strike the shore of Red Bay and see Garron Head on the far side of it. Just before reaching the Bay a spur of the hill runs down towards the road, presenting a fine cliff of red sandstone. On this hill stand the ruins gaunt and grey of the old castle of the MacDonnells already described.

A hundred yards further on an arch of sandstone spans the road, and passing through this you come upon the little village of Waterfoot. From this there is a stretch of about three miles of road on the south side of the bay to Garron Tower, which stands on the sheltered side of the Head. The house was built in 1848, by Frances Anne, Marchioness of Londonderry, daughter of the Countess of Antrim, a lady, it is said, of strongly marked character, which may be readily traced in several inscriptions that she has set up along the road and in the grounds.

There is a beautiful rose garden, and a very pretty summer house built on a point overlooking the sea, with a fragrant wood of fir trees behind it. The Tower has lately been turned into an hotel, and is a favourite resort of tourists, and of those who seek a quiet spot far from the madding crowd in the midst of exquisite scenery.

Still continuing the coast road to Larne in a deep glen which opens to the sea is situated the town of Glenarm.

It is said to have been incorporated by a charter of King John in the fourth year of his reign, but since the conquest of Ulster it has not exercised any municipal privileges. Glenarm Castle was for many years the residence of the MacDonnells, Earls of Antrim, of whom Randal MacDonnell, Marquis of Antrim, was attainted during the Protectorate. It was originally built in 1639; but the present castle was erected in the nineteenth century on the site of the former structure, of which very little remains. It is a noble, quadrangular pile, flanked at the angles with four large towers embellished with minarets.

At a short distance to the south is the great deer park, formerly enriched with stately timber and watered by a mountain torrent, which afterwards flows through the lawn; and on the left of the road to Larne is the little park, bounded by a succession of precipitous rocks, rising from the shore and forming a bold headland, round which has been carried the Antrim coast road from Larne to Ballycastle, cut through the solid rock and ten feet above high-water mark at spring tides.

Some years ago, just entering the town, the road crossed Glenarm Head, rising 600 feet to the mile at an incline of one foot in five. This was called "the path." Carriages had to be assisted from the neighbouring farm sheds with horses accustomed to the road; but a magnificent new road was planned out by Mr. John Bald in 1834, and executed at the joint expense of the Government and the county. He cut down the whole chalk cliffs along the margin of the sea, hurling the debris over as a protection against the waves, and laying the floor of the road at the base. Rounding the point is the town of Glenarm, with the turrets of the castle and its handsome barbican gate. The castle has only been the seat of the MacDonnells since 1750.

Glenarm

The village is picturesque and romantic. The fortalice of Dunluce was the original seat of the MacDonnells who wrested it from the MacQuillins. After the treachery of General Munro in 1642, who violated the rites of hospitality by seizing upon the person and castle of MacDonnell, the Earls of Antrim took up their residence at Ballymagarry, where they continued to reside till 1750, in which year the castle was accidentally burned, and ever since Glenarm Castle has been the family residence. The earl is descended from Sir Randal MacSorley MacDonnell of Dunluce, a descendant of the Lord of the Isles.

LARNE

THIS town is situated on the shore of Lough Larne, which was formerly called Olderfleet, and gave its name to a castle built on the extreme point of the promontory of Curran, which forms the small bay adjacent to the town. This fortress, under the protection of which the town arose, is supposed to have been erected by a Scottish family named Bisset, to whom a settlement on this part of the coast was granted by Henry III; and to have been subsequently improved by the English. Edward Bruce landed in Larne in 1315, with an army of 6,000 men, for the conquest of Ireland; and during the same reign Hugh Bisset forfeited his lands there by taking part in the rebellion. These were subsequently claimed in right of the same family by James MacDonnell, Lord Cantire, and after his death were granted by Queen Elizabeth during her pleasure to his son Angus, on condition that he should carry arms only under the King of England and pay annually a certain number of hanks and cattle.

Olderfleet Castle was at that time considered so important a defence against the Scots, that in 1569 it was entrusted to Sir Moyses Hill, but was dismantled in 1598. James I, in 1603, granted the entire headland to Sir Randal MacDonnell; but in 1612 gave the castle and lands to Sir Arthur Chichester, together with the right of ferry between this place and Islandmagee. During the disturbance of 1798 the town was attacked by an insurgent army from Ballymena, but the assailants were repulsed by the Tay Fencibles, assisted by the yeomanry and inhabitants.

The town is beautifully situated on the shore of Lough Larne, on the eastern coast, and is divided into the old and new towns. During the eighteenth century a very extensive trade was carried on in salt, of which large quantities, prepared here from rock salt imported from Liverpool, were sent from this port to Denmark, Norway, Sweden, Russia, and Prussia; the duties paid thereon on the average amounted to £18,000 per annum. About the middle of the eighteenth century this was the only port in the North of Ireland from which emigrant vessels sailed.

There are some remains of the ancient castle of Olderfleet on the promontory of Curran; and on the sea side, about a mile north of the town, is a cavern called the Black Cave, passing under the projecting base of a huge rock. The length of the cave, which is open at both sides, is sixty feet, and its height from three to thirty feet; the sides are formed of basaltic columns of large dimensions. On the shore of the lough near the town are some singular petrifactions of a blue colour, apparently the result of a spring issuing from a bank at high-water mark.

CARRICKFERGUS

CARRICKFERGUS, stretching along the north-western shore of Belfast Lough, is about a mile in length, and consists of the old or walled town in the centre, the Irish quarter on the west, and the Scotch quarter on the east, the last being formerly inhabited by fishermen descended from a colony driven by religious persecution from Galloway and Ayrshire about the year 1665.

Quiet and peaceful as the town is to-day, it has a history that carries us back to a remote past. Five hundred and twenty years after Christ, King Fergus is said to have built a castle here to defend his property, with a body of devoted followers. He sailed away to Scotland, and after many a hard fought fight he founded a large colony, which included, besides other territories along the coast of Scotland, the Isles and Cantire. He founded a line of Scottish kings, and from him, it is said, King James VI of Scotland and First of England claimed descent, and was specially interested to see that Ulster should be planted by men of Scotch descent.

After many years King Fergus returned from Scotland to his home, but as he sailed up Belfast Lough his vessel was wrecked on a rock in the bay, called afterwards the Rock Fergus, now known as Carrickfergus. His body was found, and buried in the adjacent abbey of Monkstown.

Another story tells that the same rock was called Carrick-na-Fairge-rock of the sea-and that it is from this name Carrickfergus was derived.

From very early times Carrickfergus had suffered from almost constant invasion, plunder, bloodshed, and burning. The castle, the church, and remains of the walls bear silent witness to the oft-told story. The castle was built by De Courcy about the year 1178. It is the only existing edifice in the kingdom which exhibits the old Norman military stronghold, and it is justly considered one of the noblest of that time now left in Ireland.

It stands on a rocky peninsula, thirty feet high, washed on three sides by the sea. Viewed from any point it presents a most picturesque appearance, with its massive walls surmounted by cannon; its ancient gateway, with flanking towers and portcullis. One tower is still known as the Lion's Den, with vaults underneath.

Carrickfergus Castle

The keep is ninety feet high, with walls nine feet thick. It is ascended by a winding staircase, with loopholes for light and air. It is five storeys high, and the lower part is used as a magazine. On the third storey a room is still named "Fergus's Dining-room" It is forty feet long, thirty-eight feet wide, and twenty-six feet high, and is a noble apartment. One inestimable boon was a well inside the building with a never-failing supply of good spring water.

De Courcy - "Princeps Ulidiæ," as Jocelyn calls him - who built the castle and reigned in Ulster like an independent king, fell into disfavour with King John, and the castle came into possession of the De Lacey family, who, in their turn being ejected, invited Edward Bruce from Scotland. He and his brother, King Robert Bruce, of Bannockburn fame, besieged the city of Carrickfergus for twelve months, and after a fierce resistance it surrendered. Then the two brothers, with an army of 20,000 men, left for further conquests, but utter desolation followed; the end was disastrous for them. Robert returned to Scotland, and Edward was killed in a battle near Dundalk; his head, along with that of Brian O'Neill, was salted, and both were sent to King Edward II at London.

Towards the end of the sixteenth century a stone wall of great strength was built round the town, which was further defended by a moat and seven towers. The Parish Church, an antiquated cruciform structure, was originally a chapel or oratory, de- pendent on a Franciscan monastery. The entrance to a subterranean passage between the two establishments is still visible under the communion table of the church. The gaol, built on the site of the above mentioned monastery, was formerly the County Antrim prison.

In the reign of Queen Elizabeth the town obtained a charter, and this was confirmed by James, who added the privilege of sending two burgesses to the Irish Parliament. In the civil wars from 1641 Carrickfergus was one of the chief places of refuge for the Protestants of the County Antrim, and on July 10th, 1642, the first Presbytery held in Ireland met there. In that year the garrison was commanded by General Munro, who, having afterwards relinquished the cause of the English Parliament, was in 1648 surprised and taken prisoner by Sir Robert Adair.

At a later period Carrickfergus was held by the soldiers of James II, but surrendered in 1689 to the forces under Schomberg, and King William himself landed here in the following year on his way to take command in the campaign terminated by the battle of the Boyne.

The quiet of the town was not again disturbed by any occurrences of historical interest until it was attacked by the French, under General Thurot, in February, 1760. The French had long meditated an invasion of this country, but their plans were completely defeated by the skill and bravery of Lord Hawke. The little squadron of Thurot reached the Irish coast on Thursday, 21st February, 1760, and entered the Bay of Carrickfergus. It consisted of three frigates, with about 600 men. Thurot, in a council of war, advised that, without attending to Carrickfergus, they should sail to Belfast; but M. De Flobert, who was at the head of the whole embarkation, differed from his colleagues, and insisted that to leave behind them such a fortified place as Carrickfergus would be against all military rules and precedents. To these arguments Thurot at length gave way, and thus was Belfast   saved from complete plunder.

On the following day Carrickfergus surrendered, and was occupied by the French. One of their officers was sent with a flag of truce and a letter to the Sovereign or Mayor of Belfast, in these terms: "Send us 30 hogsheads of wine, 40 of brandy, 60 barrels of beer, 6,000lbs of bread, and 60 buttocks. If you don't do this immediately, we intend burning Carrickfergus, afterwards to proceed to Belfast and behave there in a similar manner. "

With this request the inhabitants thought it prudent to comply, and part of the requisition was immediately sent off; but, the weather being tempestuous, the lighter could not sail down the lough that day - Saturday. In the afternoon one of the lighters, with part of the provisions, sailed, but in her passage down the river she was brought to and stopped by a tender on the road. The same day men under arms from Belfast and neighbourhood continued to arrive, and at night the total numbers amounted to at least 3,000 men. An entrenchment commenced near the Mile End Bridge was finished, and planted with some small cannon.

About nine o'clock at night a messenger arrived from Carrickfergus with a letter to the Sovereign from Mr. Fullerton, a Presbyterian minister, stating that the French, observing the provisions were stopped, had seized him and swore that if the provisions were not sent on board by eight o'clock next morning they would have him put to the sword, with the inhabitants of the town, reduce the town itself to ashes, and then march on Belfast.

To avert, if possible, the execution of this threat, early on the following morning eight or ten carts were sent off laden with provisions, but only two were suffered to proceed, the rest being stopped at the extremity of the town. On this day and the following Sunday the troops collected in Belfast, marched six miles down the shore, and remained till night, but the enemy kept close within the walls, and made preparations to embark, and soon after took their departure, so Carrickfergus was relieved.

M. Thurot, as a gentleman of Belfast wrote to his friend at Limerick, was highly provoked at missing his prey-the town of Belfast--which he declared he would have obliged to pay £50,000, besides provisions. It was this expedition which led to the enrolling of the first Volunteer Corps in Belfast, which spread so rapidly through the country and left its mark on the future history of Ireland.

BANGOR

BANGOR, situated on the south side of Belfast Lough, twelve miles east-north-east of Belfast, has a history which brings us back to very early times. There is a map of the world, Mr. Stevenson mentions, in Hereford Cathedral, 1314, which represents the world as flat and circular, its central point being the city of Jerusalem. The disc breaks into ruggedness round its circumference, entirely detached portions being the islands of the earth. On one of these, divided into two parts by a wide river and having in outline no resemblance to Ireland, are figured on the northern half two cities-Bangor and Armagh. That celebrity in the case of Bangor was due, no doubt, to the existence of the famous Abbey of regular canons founded there by St. Comgall in 558, and over which he presided fifty years, and died and was enshrined in it. Sometime subsequently to the foundation of the abbey a school was established there under the personal direction of St. Carthagus, which, in progress of time, became one of the most noted seminaries in Europe, and was resorted to by numbers of young persons of distinction from various parts, and, according to some writers, when Alfred founded or restored the University of Oxford, he sent to the great school at Bangor for professors.

In A.D. 613 the town was destroyed by fire, and in A.D 674 the abbey was burnt. At the beginning of the ninth century they suffered severely from the predatory incursions of the Danes, in one of which, about the year A.D. 818, these merciless marauders massacred the abbot and about 900 monks. In 1125 it was rebuilt by Malachy O'Morgair, then abbot, with the addition of an oratory of stone, said by St. Bernard to have been the first building of stone and lime in Ireland, and from which this place, anciently called the "Vale of Angels," derived the name of Beanchoir, now Bangor, signifying the "White Church" or "Fair Church."

The Old Abbey Church, Bangor.

Monks and students helped to build the "monastic city." Each student built his own round boothy of wood, or his square stone cell without mortar. All alike tilled the earth, and in turn ground in querns the corn needed for the school. For the rest, they lived on alms. In very early times, when the aid of animals was forbidden, they "put the yoke to their shoulders," dragged the plough, carried the harvest home on their backs; prayer, study, and labour divided the day. Their spiritual exaltation was expressed in the severe discipline and extraordinary austerities of the monastic life. In some monasteries a single meal a day was allowed - a little bread, an egg, a little milk mixed with water, or a meal of vegetables and skim milk. In all, the most extreme forms of fasting were used -fish and flesh were often wholly forbidden. On Wednesdays and Fridays no food was taken till nones; psalms, hymns, and prayers of confession and penitence were recited, with forms handed down from the early Church. The extraordinary penances, as well as the harshness of daily life, demanded an heroic spirit and singular force of physical endurance. Since the famous hermits of the African sands there had been no such examples of ascetic endurance as was practised by the monks of Ireland.

The long career of the famous abbey and college closed with the suppression of the monasteries by Henry VIII. The lands subsequently fell into the possession of the Clanaboye O'Neills, who held them till the coming of the Scots. When Sir James Hamilton came to settle at Bangor with his Scottish followers, they found a wide range of ruined buildings on the abbey site, and a hummocky waste, which had been a burying ground for nigh on a thousand years, filled with monumental stone, some of it richly carved. They levelled the waste, and made building stone of the monuments for their new church, built against an ancient tower. As this church became old it was rebuilt in the last century, and the dead lie close around its walls.

A search here for the venerable monuments of the great church and schools of Bangor is out of the question; only one fragment of a sculptured cross has survived the Scots. This was discovered doing duty as a step to a door in the churchyard wall many years ago by the late Marquis of Dufferin and Ava, and is now in the chapel of Clandeboye House.

Doubtless in the great days of the abbey and schools Bangor Bay was well known to seafaring people as the busy place of arrival of merchant ships bearing supplies for the great monastery and schools, but after the suppression of the monasteries the little town must have decreased in size. The country round was wild. In the woods deer were numerous, and the author of the "Montgomery Manuscripts" mentions wolves in the list of animals hunted by the Viscount Montgomery. But the Hamilton settlers quickly changed the aspect of the place, and the thrifty, busy Scots soon made a new Bangor.

Of the ancient abbey there is but little left. A wall about 90 feet in length, 16 feet in height, and 3 feet thick-probably a part of Malachy O'Morgair's twelfth-century church-is all that is visible. The ancient burying-ground extended far beyond the limits of the enclosure in which the old church now stands. It included the ground which, has been for very many years the rectory grounds.

Not until 1865 was the railway from Holy wood to Bangor opened; from that time the increase in size and population of Bangor became rapid. The population is now about 8,000. The great attractions of the place at the present time are its pure air and sea, and its unrivalled facilities for bathing and boating. Bangor is the headquarters of the Royal Ulster Yacht Club. The club's annual two-days' regatta is one of the most important yachting events in Ireland, and attracts all the best boats in British waters.

Newcastle

ONE who wrote in 1757 tells of a house and well improved demesne of Edward Matthews, Esq., which formerly belonged to Magennis, Lord Iveagh, and was forfeited in the rebellion of 1641 and granted to William Hawkins of London, Esq. The castle was built by Felix Magennis in the year 1588, as appears by an inscription on a stone over the front door.

As it exists today, Newcastle is of modern origin. In the turbulent times that lasted through so many centuries, the beauty of the scenery and purity of the air called to men in vain. The fastnesses of the mountain formed, no doubt, a safe refuge for the outlaw-a secure eyrie whence bands of marauders could descend on the rich lands of Lecale; so, to protect their property, the powerful Magennis family erected a stronghold at Newcastle, selecting for its site the point where the Shimna river debouches into the sea. Felix Magennis appears to have selected the site of an older structure, as mention is made in "The Annals of the Four Masters" of a castle here as early as 1433. Like so many of the ancient fortresses, the site chosen so as to command a ford - the ford afterwards known as "fearsat na chaislein nui"- the ford of the new castle, which crossed the mouth of the Shimna river where now the broad new bridge stands. The castle which gave its name to the town exists no longer.

The soil about Newcastle towards the sea is sandy, and abounds with rabbits-more onward it is rocky and hard. It is remarkable for health and old age.

It is still famous for the beauty of its scenery, the invigorating purity of its air, its facilities for mountain climbing, bathing, golfing, or sketching. The houses of the town sweep round the sandy shore of the Bay of Dundrum for more than a mile northward beyond the railway station and Slieve Donard Hotel; the broad beach curves away for miles, backed by the dunes that the golfer knows so well.

The present population of Newcastle is returned as 1,765. The Moneycarragh river, which flows into Dundrum Bay a couple of miles north of Newcastle, affords plenty of small brown trout with an occasional good one. Golf is perhaps the attraction that now draws visitors from a distance to Newcastle. The sanddunes that stretch from the railway station northward for several miles are an ideal place for this ancient game, and the Royal County Down Golf Club have made their headquarters here. Their handsome and commodious club-house stands within two hundred yards of the Slieve Donard Hotel.

Newcastle

ROSTREVOR AND WARRENPOINT

ROSTREVOR is a placid, restful little town. Its surroundings are very picturesque; the wide waters of the bay, with the mountains of Carlingford in the distance, and the rugged slopes of the Mourne mountains on the landward side. Cold and frost do not linger long here. It has also all the advantages of a seaside resort-good bathing, fishing, and boating. A little way outside the town a zig-zag path leads to Cloughmore ("Cloch Mor," the big stone), a celebrated erratic block of granite about 30 tons weight that stands on a shoulder of the mountain overlooking Rostrevor, at an elevation of 957 feet. The path zig-zags through the wood, and, emerging on the open hillside, passes the shepherd's hut, and reaches the great boulder that: the champion Finn MacCool threw across the lough from Carlingford mountain! Geologists prefer to attribute its present: position to the action of the ice during the glacial period. The composition of the stone proves that it came from the northward, from the neighbourhood of Newry; the glacial strata in the neighbourhood show that there was a general ice flow from this direction. Rostrevor is in the parish of Kilbroney. The name is derived from its patron saint, " Bronach," a virgin of Glain-Seichis, as she is described in the calendar of the

O'Clerys. The ruins of the ancient parish church, though not, of course, the primitive structure raised by St. Bronach, still occupy the original site in the valley in which she has impressed her name, some half-mile from the village of Rostrevor, They consist of a nave and chancel, smothered in ivy. In the south-east corner of the graveyard stands a fine early cross of granite, set in a large, roughly-squared block of the same rock. To the west is the ancient well of St. Brigid. This old parish church must have shared the fate of most of the churches of the diocese in the rebellion of 1641, since it is described in an official return made during the Commonwealth as "out of repair." It was doubtless repaired again, but in 1733 it fell into ruin.

Rostrevor has an ancient history, and has borne many names. The oldest name is Carrigavaghad; it was also called Castle Roe, and finally Rostrevor. The massive castle, once the stronghold of Rory Magennis, one of the Lords of Iveagh, stood near the centre of the town, but now no vestige of it is left.

In the reign of Queen Elizabeth the place passed into the hands of Sir Marmaduke Whitechurch. Madame Mary Lowry tells the story of that old romance. The chieftain of Magennis, and the rightful Lord of Iveagh, was outlawed from his home, and a price put upon his head. Sir Marmaduke Whitechurch was made owner of the estate, and lived in the ancestral home of Castle Roe. Magennis loved Sir Marmaduke's fair daughter Eva, but his suit seemed hopeless. One evening, as he was in a boat on the lough, the old boatman told him that night was falling, and spoke of the danger of passing Castle Roe. He knew that if any of Sir Marmaduke's men caught sight of his enemy near the castle he would soon adorn the highest tree in the forest; but the young chieftain was in a reckless mood, so he landed at the little cove and wandered on to the castle, which was the dearest spot on earth to him, and was filled with recollections of the past. Now it was the home of his beloved Eva. The moon was shining softly through the long rows of stately trees. He scaled the rampart of the castle at a remote corner, and every window was dark but one which looked upon a lawn. Since he was a little child he had not entered his father's halls or passed the boundary wall. At the open window sat Rose Whitechurch and young Edward Trevor, who was a favourite captain of Queen Elizabeth, and afterwards Baron of Dungannon. They were to be married next morning.

Sir Marmaduke sat further from the window, with the light from the torches falling on his grey hair and handsome face, while close beside him sat his youngest and best-loved daughter, Eva. "To-morrow, Rose," he said, "you leave this place for ever; wood and mountain, hill and valley, sea and sequestered glen, you know and love so well, will know you no more." "Oh, say not so, father,", she cried, could not bear the thought of leaving Castle Roe and all its charms for ever." "Look out, Trevor, and you, too, Eva. See, the moon touches the tree-tops with her silver light and tinges the faint outline of the cliffs of Carlingfrod. See there on the broad breast of Slieve Ban, where Cloughmore sits, a feathery cloud rests like a crown upon her brow. Where can the eye take in at one glance so much ? Oh! it is as beautiful as ----" "Yourself," exclaimed the enraptured lover. "Aye, Rose, as you and Trevor," interrupted Sir Marmaduke. "From this night on it shall no more be known as Castle Roe, but it shall be called Rose Trevor" (Rostrevor)

Rostrevor.

Magenins waited long, but could not get a chance of speech with Eva. The next night he braved the Walls again, and was taken prisoner. He heard Eva entreating her father to spare his life, and he, with stern voice, swore that the next morning would see him hung from the highest tree. Shut in the dungeon keep, there seemed no hope left, but Eva came in the night and set him free. She fled with him, and there, on the rugged brow of Slieve Mor. they were joined in holy wedlock by the waiting priest. For two years they lived in perfect happiness, as only those who live for each other know, but death had marked the gentle Eva for his own, and now a granite-covered grave marks her resting-place in Kilbroney.

Some majestic yew trees flourish near the ancient walls, and the tower of the old church is a mass of ivy. Kilbroney had a famous bell called "Clogh- ban," the "White Bell," which was known all over the country. Once, when invasion threatened in the old turbulent times, and danger came very near, the precious bell was carefully hidden and safely kept. The danger passed, and, in later years, when the new generation wanted the bell, it could not be found. Those who had hidden it had kept the secret so well that when they died it remained a secret still. It became a proverb in the country, and people used to say in sceptical tones, "It will happen when Kilbroney bell rings again."

A great many years passed. One night a terrible storm raged in Kilbroney, and through the pauses, when the wind seemed to wait to gather strength for a more violent blast, there was distinctly heard the full clear sound of a bell ringing. All through that awful night it rang, and when morning came and the storm was over it was still heard in tones, now high, now low, but full of music. The frightened people came near. There, in the ancient tower, was the famous bell. It had never been anywhere else, for the old monks had built it in with stones, and no one had ever thought of looking for it there. As years passed away the tower was covered with ivy, and clinging tendrils had held the stones together until the storm had swept the ivy away.

When the stones fell down the bell was once more free to swing to and fro, as it had done hundreds of years before. It was removed from the roofless ruined building and was placed in the new chapel, where it is used every Sunday morning as the altar bell.

A succession of pretty villa residences fringes the road from Rostrevor to Warrenpoint. The leading feature of this popular little town is its fine promenade fronting the sea for half a mile, and from which there is a fine view of the lough and the Carlingford and Mourne mountains. At the beginning of the last century Warrenpoint consisted of a few houses; now it has a population of 2,000, rising in the summer months to 5,000. Good boating and bathing may be had, and for golfers there is an eighteen-hole course, with a dainty little club-house.